Indian Fire Ritual

Indian Fire Ritual

MUSASHI TACHIKAWA
SHRIKANT BAHULKAR
MADHAVI KOLHATKAR

Foreword

C. G. KASHIKAR

MOTILAL BANARSIDASS PUBLISHERS
PRIVATE LIMITED • DELHI

First Edition: Delhi, 2001

ISBN: 81-208-1781-8

Also available at:

MOTILAL BANARSIDASS

236, 9th Main III Block, Jayanagar, Bangalore 560 011
41 U.A. Bungalow Road, Jawahar Nagar, Delhi 110 007
8 Mahalaxmi Chamber, Warden Road, Mumbai 400 026
120 Royapettah High Road, Mylapore, Chennai 600 004
Sanas Plaza, 1302 Baji Rao Road, Pune 411 002
8 Camac Street, Kolkata 700 017
Ashok Rajpath, Patna 800 004
Chowk, Varanasi 221 001

Printed in India

BY JAINENDRA PRAKASH JAIN AT SHRI JAINENDRA PRESS,
A-45 NARAINA, PHASE-I, NEW DELHI 110 028
AND PUBLISHED BY NARENDRA PRAKASH JAIN FOR
MOTILAL BANARSIDASS PUBLISHERS PRIVATE LIMITED,
BUNGALOW ROAD, DELHI 110 007

Table of Contents

Foreword

India's contact with the outer world developed in the eighteenth century A.D. It brought a new awakening among the Indian Society, and shed new light on the understanding of India's old tradition. Some of the officers of the East India Company of England who came to India for the progressive administration of Indian territories themselves learnt the Sanskrit language with great effort and discovered the hidden treasure of culture and philosophical knowledge. They managed to transport to Europe and America Sanskrit manuscripts of classical philosophical and religious literature including the Vedic religion. This resulted into the publication of scientific and historical studies pertaining to hundreds of texts. The Vedic religion and literature drew attention of a number of scholars. As a result, critical editions, translations and cultural historical studies were published.

There have been scholars who dived deep into the intricacies of ritualistic religions. It was really creditable that they succeeded in understanding the complicated rites simply through a close study of the text with or without commentaries belonging to a tradition totally foreign to them. In the course of time, it was felt that the witnessing of actual performance of various rituals would help a fuller understanding. Many a scholar consequently visited India, and availed themselves of the opportunities to personally attend such performances with great efforts. This has had a favourable effect on a deeper study of the Vedic ritualistic religion which ultimately contributes to the scientific knowledge of religion in general.

In this connection, the study of the Vedic ritual, namely Pavitreṣṭi, presented in the following pages by Dr. Musashi Tachikawa, Dr. Shrikant Bahulkar and Dr. Madhavi Kolhatkar on the basis of the actual performance deserves appreciation.

The Pavitreṣṭi has first been described in the *Prāyaścitta* section of the *Baudhāyana Śrautasūtra* (28.2), the oldest of the *Śrautasūtras*, which belongs to the *Taittirīya* recension of the *Kṛṣṇa Yajurveda*. The *Baudhāyana Śrautasūtra* is mainly a *pravacana* representing the oral discourses delivered by the Ācārya. To the original discourses were added certain portions by the followers of the school, and the *Prāyaścitta* section belongs to such portions. Even then it is much old. Basically the Pavitreṣṭi was an expiatory rite to be performed by an Āhitāgni in case he went on a journey alone for a period less than a year, while his sacred fires were maintained and worshipped at home by his wife. This Iṣṭi was also regarded as an optional sacrifice to be performed for allaying some deficiency. As the word denotes, the Iṣṭi aims at achieving purification in some form. Its performance for a number of consecutive days imports power to remove evil of generations together.

This Iṣṭi is prescribed also in a few other *Śrautasūtras* belonging to the *Taittirīya* recension. Thus, the *Vādhūla Śrautasūtra* which is almost as old as the *Baudhāyana Śrautasūtra* has prescribed this Iṣṭi (XII.5). The Pavitreṣṭi prescribed by Vādhūla is intended for removing some deficiency--ritualistic or otherwise. Vādhūla has not mentioned the deficiency caused by going on a journey for a period less than a year. The *Bhāradvāja Śrautasūtra,* a senior contemporary of the *Āpastamba Śrautasūtra* has described the Pavitreṣṭi in its supplementary portion (*Pariśeṣasūtras* 189-201). Its performance aims at removing impurity occurred in some form. The same *Sūtra*-text (*sūtras* 202-209) has prescribed the Atipavitreṣṭi in which additional offerings have been prescribed. This Iṣṭi is prescribed for the fulfilment of a positive desire. It may be performed by an Āhitāgni who has gone on a journey for a period more than a year, having his sacred fires at home. It may also be performed for general purification. The *Āśvalāyana Śrautasūtra* (II.13) has prescribed the Pavitreṣṭi for one going on a journey for a period over a year. No other *Śrautasūtra* has prescribed the Pavitreṣṭi or Atipavitreṣṭi. Rudradatta in his commentary on *Āpastamba Śrautasūtra* (VI.26) has mentioned these two Iṣṭis prescribed in the *Bhāradvāja Pariśeṣasūtra.*

Thus the Pavitreṣṭi which is not described in any *Brāhmāa* text, is prescribed in some *Śrautasūtras* for achieving purification in some form. The variations in their forms can be explained on chronological grounds.

It is customary among the ritual texts to adopt, from other Vedic texts, ritual which is absent in one's own Vedic school. The Pavitreṣṭi is an instance of this custom. Barring a single instance of the optional sacrifice called Mitravindeṣṭi, the *Śukla Yajurveda* (*Mantra, Śatapatha Brāhmāa* and the *Kātyāyana Śrautasūtra*) has not prescribed any optional performance. The Pavitreṣṭi is therefore not prescribed in the *Śukla Yajurveda* recension. The followers of this recension thought it expedient to borrow the Pavitreṣṭi-ritual from the *Baudhāyana Śrautasūtra.* The *Baudhāyana* school, the oldest one, had an honoured place among the followers of the other Vedic schools. In the field of the domestic rites, the Udakaśānti prescribed in a supplement to the *Baudhāyana Ģhyasūtra* has been traditionally adopted by the followers of all Vedic schools.

From the *Mantra-Brāhmāa* down to the manuals of the various Vedic schools, it is observed that the procedure of the rituals and expiatory rites have undergone modifications under the influence of geographical, social and economic conditions. Even more modifications have occurred in the present days. The editors of the present work have carefully noted such changes. The ritual tradition is fast disappearing in India. It is therefore imperative to record whatever of it is available at present so that such records may provide material necessary for compiling the cultural history of India.

Studies in Indology took root in Japan particularly in the nineteenth century A.D. It is gratifying to find that the tradition is going on. The traditions would go a long way in promoting the study of comparative religion and cultural history of Japan. The editors therefore deserve congratulations for contributing their mite towards that end.

C. G. Kashikar

TILAK MAHARASHTRA VIDYAPEETH, PUNE
August 15, 1997.
Independence Day.

Preface

This book illustrates the Pavitreṣṭi ritual performed in the Vaidika Saṃśodhana Maṇḍala, Pune, Maharashtra, India, on the morning of the 27th July, 1979. The Pavitreṣṭi ritual is a modified form of the Darśapūrṇamāsa (the New Moon and the Full Moon sacrifice) which is one of the most basic Vediç rituals. Nowadays, however, it is difficult to observe Vedic rituals being performed, because they have become almost obsolete. A number of Śrauta texts explain the procedures of the Darśapūrṇamāsa and other Vedic rituals fully, but they fail to give a clear image of the priests' gestures and of the ritual utensils to those who live outside India. Therefore, in the spring of 1979, M. Tachikawa asked S. Bahulkar to arrange matters so that we could have a chance to observe a Vedic ritual being performed. At the request of S. Bahulkar a team of priests then came from Nasik to perform the Pavitreṣṭi ritual in Pune.

Here we wish to express our deepest gratitude to the priests who performed the ritual and permitted us to photograph it. We must thank the Vaidika Saṃśodhana Maṇḍala for allowing us to use the main hall for the performance of the ritual. We also thank those ex-students of the Department of Indian Philosophy of the Nagoya University who were staying in Pune at that time and helped us in taking records of the ritual : Dr. Yūkō Miyasaka photographed the ritual; except Nos. 1-9, 34, 39, 41, 48, 55, 60, 74, and 150-154, which were taken by M. Tachikawa. Dr. Shoun Hino was engaged in taking the 8m.m. movie film of the ritual. Miss

Mitsue Iwai and Mr. Kuniharu Hōjō recorded the priests' recitations of the Mantras. Miss Yūko Yagami drew the illustrations by tracing the photographs.

In summer of 1981, M. Tachikawa was given the chance to read the *Kātīyeṣṭidīpaka,* which describes the procedure of the Darśapūrṇamāsa, under the guidance of the late Dr. Vidyadhar Bhide of the University of Pune, who had participated in the performance of the Pavitreṣṭi as a Sadasya. Without his initiating Tachikawa in Śrauta studies, this book would not have seen the light of the day. From 1986, M. Kolhatkar started to work on this book.

Prof. C. G. Kashikar, spared no pains in going through the manuscript of this book, made valuable suggestions and was kind enough to write the foreword. The Bhandarkar Oriental Research Institute kindly permitted us to reproduce the manuscript in their possession, on which the performance of the Pavitreṣṭi was based. Shri Abhay Pathak of Abhay Mudranalaya diligently carried out the complicated work of the typesetting. Shri. N. P. Jain of Motilal Banarsidass readily accepted the book for publication. We are grateful to all of them and also others who participated--directly or indirectly--in the performance of the ritual and offered their help in bringing out this book.

Musashi Tachikawa
National Museum of Ethnology
Osaka, JAPAN.

Shrikant Bahulkar
Tilak Maharashtra Vidyapeeth,
Pune, India.

Madhavi Kolhatkar
Deccan College, Pune, India.

Introduction

The Structure of Pavitreṣṭi

In ancient India, the fire ceremony was performed as the basic part of the Vedic ritual which continued in the post-Vedic tradition--generally called Hindu tradition--in a modified form. Although not great in number, there are also some instances in which Vedic rituals have, with the addition of some Hindu elements, been preserved in a form close to that of ancient times.

Here we shall undertake an examination and analysis of one of the Vedic rituals. The rite with which we shall deal here cannot be described as a complete re-enactment of that ancient Vedic ritual, nor is there any need to maintain it in that manner. We should rather first take note of the fact that even if it was simplified in later times and did incorporate some non-solemn elements, the traditions of this rite have been preserved for approximately three thousand years virtually in the manner laid down in the ritual texts.

A considerable amount of literature relating to Vedic ritual has been preserved down to the present day, and the volume of translations of this literature into European languages is also quite large. But for people living outside India, it is difficult to draw mental picture of altars and utensils that they have never seen and to understand the actions performed during a rite simply by reading the ritual texts. In what follows we shall endeavour to deepen our understanding of a typical rite that has been performed in India since ancient times through the use of photographs of its actual performance in contemporary India.

The fire ceremony, basic to Vedic ritual, was also eventually incorporated into Tantric Buddhism, and the *homa* rite thus absorbed by Indian Mahāyāna Buddhism was disseminated throughout Nepal, Tibet, China and Japan. In the course of this it continues to be performed in Tibet, Nepal and Japan. For an understanding of the structure of Buddhist *homa* too, the knowledge of the structure of *homa* as it was performed in ancient India is indispensable.

The Vedic ritual is described in an orderly form in the ceremonial guides called *Kalpa-Sūtras* pertaining to the various schools of the Vedas. The sacrifices are : (i) obligatory *(nitya)*, to be performed daily or on certain days of the lunar calender throughout the life, as a cycle of rituals; (ii) incidental *(naimittika)*, to be performed on certain events; (iii) optional *(kāmya)*, performed for special ends and (iv) expiatory *(prāyaścitta)*, to be performed in the case of any ritualistic deficiency. Moreover, the sacrifices are divided into two groups : (i) *Śrauta* i.e., the sacrifices described in the *Śruti*, viz., the *Saṃhitā* and the *Brāhmaṇa* and dealt with in the *Śrauta-Sūtras*, a part of the *Kalpa-Sūtras;* and (ii) *Gṛhya* 'domestic rites', otherwise called *Smārta* based on *Smṛti* 'remembrance', laid down in the *Gṛhya-Sūtras*, another part of the *Kalpa-Sūtras*.

The prominent Śrauta sacrifices are counted as seven Havis-sacrifices consisted of the oblations such as clarified butter *(ājya)* or sacrificial cake *(puroḍāśa)* and seven Soma-sacrifices with the oblations of the Soma-juice. The animal-sacrifice is also performed in some of the sacrifices. There is a similar grouping of the domestic rites *(pāka)* too.

The Darśapūrṇamāsa sacrifice forms one of the seven Havis-sacrifices. According to the order of time, it comes after the Agnyādheya 'setting up of the three sacred fires', namely, Gārhapatya, Āhavanīya and Dakṣiṇa and the Agnihotra 'daily offerings to the sacred fires'. However, the *Śrautasūtras* commence the description of the sacrifices with that of the Darśapūrṇamāsa, for this sacrifice is a model *(prakṛti)* of the type of sacrifices called

Iṣṭi. The other sacrifices styled after the model are 'modifications' *(vikṛti)* which include various oblations offered to different deities for various ends.

The word Darśapūrṇamāsa means an Iṣṭi to be performed on the new moon day *(darśa)* and the full moon day *(pūrṇamāsa)*. It is a kind of obligatory sacrifice *(nitya)*; nevertheless, it can be performed also for the accomplishment of various desires with an addition of certain offerings. Though it is called the New Moon and the Full Moon sacrifice, the former is performed on the day when the full moon day and the first day of the dark half of the month *(pratipad)* are joined, and the latter on the combination *(sandhi)* of the new moon day and the first day of the bright half of the month. According to the tradition of the *Śukla Yajurveda*, the sacrifice is performed on the day in which the fourteenth day *(caturdaśī)* and the last day of the fortnight *(paurṇamāsī or amāvāsyā)* are joined. The performance occupies two days, i.e., the full moon day and the first day and the new moon day and the first day *(pratipad)*. On the full moon day and the new moon day, some preliminary rites are performed and the main sacrifice is performed on the subsequent day. The Full Moon sacrifice may be compressed into one day; in that case, the whole sacrifice is performed on the *pratipad*.

The sacrificer is the one who has set up the three sacred fires *(agnyādhāna)* and is engaged in the daily offerings to them *(agnihotra)*. He should begin the performance from the first Full Moon Day that comes after the setting up of the sacred fires. First, he performs an Iṣṭi called Anvārambhaṇīyā and then proceeds to the Pūrṇamāsa.

For the performance he selects four priests, viz., the Hotṛ, the Adhvaryu, the Āgnīdhra and the Brahman. Here it would not be out of context to explain, in brief, the duties of the priests in the Śrauta ritual. In the Śrauta sacrifices, there are four groups of priests, each consisting of four. The Hotṛ is the chief priest among those belonging to the Ṛgveda. The Adhvaryu is the leader of the priests of the Yajurveda. To the Sāmaveda pertain the Udgātṛ and the other three priests. The fourth group is of the Brahman and the others. The Brahman may belong to any Veda. It is the tradition of the Atharvaveda that insists that the Brahman should belong to that Veda. However, this injunction would generally be followed by the sacrificer who belongs to the Atharvaveda. The Hotṛ recites mantras from the Ṛgveda. The Adhvaryu performs the major part of the acts in the sacrifice along with the recitation of the mantras from the Yajurveda. In the Darśapūrṇamāsa sacrifices, there is no role for the priest of the Sāmaveda; the sacrifice is performed by the priests of the Ṛgveda and the Yajurveda only. The Āgnīdhra belongs to the group of the Brahman; his duty is almost like that of an attendant. The Brahman is required to be the most learned one in the Vedic lore. He observes silence while the mantras are being recited and superintends the actions. His permission is asked by the Adhvaryu before doing some of the acts. The sacrificer and his wife also take part in certain rites. Many of the rites are followed by the subsequent recitation *(anumantraṇa)* by the sacrificer.

The first day of the performance is called *upavasatha* on which the deities are presumed to have arrived and the second one *yajanīya* 'the day of the principal offerings' In the morning, the sacrificer, after having offered his daily offerings to the sacred fires *(agnihotra),* begins the ritual of the Darśapūrṇamāsa. He should have his head and chin shaved and nails pared. He and his wife take bath and sit to the west of the Gārhapatya fire. They declare their intention to perform the sacrifice. This is called *saṅkalpa* 'announcement.' The sacrificer formally chooses the four priests. The Adhvaryu then adds three firesticks to each of the three sacred fires. This is called *anvādhāna* 'adding fuel to the fires.' He goes out of the sacrificial ground--to the east or to the north--and fetches bundles of sacrificial grass *(barhis)* and faggot *(idhma).* The first handful of grass he cuts is called *prastara.* He cuts three or more odd-numbered handfuls of grass to be strewn within the altar. The sacrificial faggot consists of twenty-one sticks. He returns by the same way he goes and keeps the sacrificial grass and faggot towards the north of the Gārhapatya fire. He also prepares a brush of *darbha* blades called *veda*. He asks the Āgnīdhra, or someone to strew the *darbha* grass around the sacred fires or he does the act by himself. If the performance is for two days, on the full moon day, the *anvādhāna* and strewing of the grass are performed and on the next day is done the fetching of sacrificial grass and faggot, making of the *veda*-bunch and other rites. If the sacrifice is compressed into one day, the strewing of the grass is done after the making of the *veda*-bunch. The sacrificer takes meal in the noon and observes fast after that.

The Darśapūrṇamāsa is said to be the prototype or model *(prakṛti)* of all other Iṣṭis--obligatory, occasional and optional as well. Among the modifications *(vikṛti)* of the Darśapūrṇamāsa, there is an Iṣṭi known as Pavitreṣṭi "an Iṣṭi that brings about purification." It is regarded to be a rite for the atonement or expiation of sins *(prāyaścitta)*, but it may be performed as an optional one in order to fulfil certain desires *(kāmya)*.

The Pavitreṣṭi performed in Pune in 1979 was performed by the priests from Nasik, coming to Pune for that very purpose. Hence it was decided to perform it in one day without the *upavasatha* rites. Since the Pavitreṣṭi, is modelled after the Pūrṇamāseṣṭi, it was performed on the first day *(pratipad)* of the dark half of the month.

The general procedure of the Pavitreṣṭi

The procedure followed in the Darśapūrṇamāsa, which has been repeatedly performed for as long as three thousand years, is truly elaborate and possesses a remarkable structure. Stated in general terms, the preliminary rites are performed in the first half and the main rites follow in the second half. In the first half the ritual utensils are sacralized, the offerings are prepared and the altar is constructed. Then follow the principal offerings (*pradhāna*) in the second half, the subsequent offerings are made in the fire within the altar. The oblations may be divided into the principal offerings and two additional sets of offerings that precede it and follow it. A more detailed overview of the structure of this ritual is given below. It may be noted that the Pavitreṣṭi which we witnessed in July 1979 began at 7.30 a.m. and ended at 11.40 a.m. In the following outline we have also added the time at which each stage began.

Since the contents of the Darśapūrṇamāsa are virtually identical to that of the Pavitreṣṭi, it is possible to infer the temporal scope of the former on the basis of the time that was required for the performance of the latter.

Procedure of the Pavitreṣṭi

0.	**Priests, Utensils and Preparation**		
1.	**Preliminary Rites**		**Time**
1.1	Vitalization of the fire		7:45
1.2	Fetching the holy water		8:39
1.3	Preparation of the sacrificial cakes		
	1.3.1	Measuring the oblation material	8:41
	1.3.2	Sacralization of the water	8:42
	1.3.3	Sacralization of the oblation material and utensils	8:45
	1.3.4	Making the sacrificial cakes	8:49
1.4	Construction of the altar (*vedikaraṇa*)		
	1.4.1	Digging up the ground and marking out the altar	9:46
	1.4.2	Cleansing the utensils	9:53
	1.4.3	Girdling the sacrificer's wife	9:55

The structure of the Pavitreṣṭi

We shall now examine the structure of the Pavitreṣṭi on the basis of the ritual procedure mentioned above.

1. Preliminary Rites

As noted earlier, in the preliminary rites performed during the first half of the ritual, preparations are made for the *homa*, or offerings, to be performed in the second half of the ritual. An important notion underlying these rites is the sacralization of the oblation material, utensils and altar.

1.1 *Vitalization of the Fire* (Figs. 26-34)

A brahmin who establishes and maintains the three sacred fires is called an *Agnihotrin.* The fire used in an Iṣṭi such as the Darśapūrṇamāsa or Pavitreṣṭi is the one that has been kept alive by an Āhitāgni in the hearth of his house.

On the occasion of the Pavitreṣṭi that we observed in 1979, the fire was produced by rubbing together two pieces of wood called *araṇī.* This was because the priests had come to Pune from their hometown Nasik, with the fire consigned in the *araṇis.*

1.2 *Fetching the Holy Water* (Fig. 35)

After the morning Agnihotra has been offered, the water used for sacralization is "led forward," to the altar. This water is called *praṇītā* or 'that which has been led forward', and it subsequently plays an important role throughout the performance. It is carried in a rectangular, wooden vessel furnished with a small handle and is placed to the north of the Āhavanīya fire.

1.3 *Preparation of the Sacrificial Cakes*

The two kinds of oblations to the deities in the Pavitreṣṭi are baked cakes made of kneaded rice flour and the clarified butter.

1.3.1 *Measuring the Oblation Material* (Figs. 36-37)

At this point, when the fire is blazing and the holy water has been fetched, the priests commence preparing the sacrificial cakes. They begin by measuring the grains (*havis*)--in actual practice, rice or rice flour--used for making the sacrificial cakes. The Adhvaryu places a small ladle called *agnihotrahavaṇī* in the winnowing basket that is placed on the ground near the Gārhapatya fire. Two blades of *darbha* grass called "strainers" are then placed across the ladle, and the rice (or rice flour) is poured out by means of the ladle with the strainers. The *darbha* grass is believed to be endowed with sacralizing power, and this action represents a type of filtration,

On the occasion of the Pavitreṣṭi in 1979, rice flour had already been placed in a metal vessel, but according to the ancient texts the paddy should be brought to the ritual site in a small cart from which the priest should take the necessary amount. Sacralization by means of water was then performed not on the entire quantity of paddy contained in the cart, but only on the amount that had been measured out.

1.3.2 *Sacralization of the Water* (Figs. 38-40)

The Adhvaryu scoops up with a spoon some water from the vessel containing the *praṇītā*-water and pours it into the *agnihotrahavaṇī* and sacrifices that water by means of two *darbha* blades called "strainers" and places those "strainers" over the water. He sprinkles the water three times with the water in the same ladle by means of the hand with the palm turned upwards.

1.3.3 *Sacralization of the Oblation Material and Utensils* (Figs. 41-42)

Now that the water has been "led forward" and sacralized by means of the same water, the ingredients of the sacrificial cakes that have already been measured out and the utensils that are necessary for making the cakes are sacralized with the water that has just been sacralized. This is done three times by means of the hand with the palm turned upwards.

1.3.4 *Making the Sacrificial Cakes* (Figs. 43-57)

Insofar as the rice for making the sacrificial cakes has been measured, the preparation of the sacrificial cakes may be said to have already begun. But now that the sacralization of the water and utensils has been completed, the rite of making sacrificial cakes commences.

The Adhvaryu places a small amount of paddy in a small mortar (*ulūkhala*) and goes through the motions of pounding the paddy with a small pestle (*musala*). In the case of the Pavitreṣṭi in 1979, rice flour had been prepared in advance, and this was used from the stage when the ingredients were measured out. But during the ritual, the process of pounding the rice (*haviḥkaṇḍana*), husking the paddy (*nistuṣīkaraṇa*), and pulverising the rice grains (*taṇḍulapeṣaṇa*) is performed ritually.

When the rice has ritually been made into flour, and taken into a pan, the priests add some water from the *praṇītā*-vessel and some hot water called "rejoicing one" *(madantī)* in the flour, knead it, and make five cakes about the size of the palm of the hand. The number of cakes is related to the number of deities to whom offerings are to be made during the ritual, and in this case the number five represents half of ten, the number of deities to whom offerings are made in the Pavitreṣṭi; the remaining five deities are offered clarified butter.

The sacrificial cakes are baked on the Gārhapatya fire. In the Pavitreṣṭi of 1979, they placed them on an earthen potsherd marked with several lines and then baked. Originally, that is to say in the Vedic ritual of ancient time, it was not a single potsherd that was used; instead, a number of small pieces of potsherds were arranged in the manner of a jigsaw so as to make a collective unit. The lines on the surface of the present-day earthen potsherd may be regarded as representing the joints of these former potsherds.

1.4 *Construction of the Altar (vedikaraṇa)*

While the sacrificial cakes are being baked on the Gārhapatya fire, the priests begin constructing the altar. On the occasion of the *Pavitreṣṭi* in 1979, however, the altar had already been constructed with earth, bricks and cowdung on the day prior to the performance of the ritual (i.e. 26th July), and even in cases when the Āhitāgni performs the Darśapūrṇamāsa at his house in Nasik the hearths are already in place, although they have not yet been sacralized.

1.4.1 *Digging Up the Ground and Marking Out the Altar* (Figs. 58-65)

The word *vedi* refers to the sacrificial altar in a broad sense of the term. It is not, however, an elevated altar as one might expect, but is practically at the same level of the surrounding area. The earth is dug a little and solidified so as to make gradual slope towards the north-east. The *vedi* of the ritual site at the home of the Āhitāgni in Nasik was made of stones placed at a depth of 7-8 centimeters below the surrounding ground.

Immediately after the fire has been produced by means of the *araṇis,* three sides of the Āhavanīya fire are enclosed by three enclosing sticks, and then the ground for the *vedi* is dug up. This act is done only symbolically.

One function of the *vedi* is to serve as a depositary for clarified butter and sacrificial cakes and for utensils such as ladles. Prior to the completion of the *vedi,* the offerings and utensils are placed outside the *vedi,* but after the *darbha* grass has been spread over the *vedi* and the *vedi* has been sacralized, they are placed on the top of the *darbha* grass.

The procedure for the ritual construction of the *vedi* is as follows : First the length of the 'shoulders' and then the length of the 'buttocks' is measured. The shape of the *vedi* would appear to represent the upper half of a woman's body. The part on the east side where the sacrificial fire is situated is called the 'shoulders', while the part in the west, towards the Gārhapatya fire and where the Adhvaryu sits, is called the 'buttocks'.

Next the Āgnīdhra prepares a 'rubbish pit' (*utkara*) to the north of the Āhavanīya fire. Then the Adhvaryu, chanting mantras, takes some blades of *darbha* grass and a wooden sword, transfers them to his left hand, and then chants a mantra while touching the wooden sword with his right hand.

The Adhvaryu next places a blade of *darbha* grass on the *vedi* and strikes the ground either below the grass or from above it. He then places the earth that has been--or is supposed to have been--dug up on a small round plate and looks fixedly at the spot from which the earth has been taken. The earth is then discharged on the above-mentioned rubbish pit.

The above actions are repeated three times, signifying that the ground where the *vedi* is to be constructed is dug up. But because its outline is not yet clear, the act of demarcation is to be performed.

The Adhvaryu says to the Brahman, "I shall now undertake the first 'tracing' (*parigraha*)," whereupon the Brahman grants him permission. The Adhvaryu then traces the outline of the site of the *vedi* with a pointed stick called *abhri*. This represents the first demarcation of the *vedi*, and it is performed a second time in the same manner.

1.4.2 *Cleansing of the Utensils* (Fig. 66)

As a result of the above actions the ground for the altar (*vedi*) has been ritually dug up, and its contours have also been ritually demarcated. Next, the priests purify the utensils, sacralize the sacrificer's wife, and spread *darbha* grass over the altar. With these actions the tracing of the altar is completed and it becomes a place suitable for arranging the sacrificial cakes and placing the ladles to be used for the clarified butter.

The Adhvaryu now heats the ladles over the Gārhapatya fire, and he purifies them by touching each with *darbha* grass. He then sprinkles each ladle with some of the water that has already been sacralized.

1.4.3 *Girdling the Sacrificer's Wife* (Figs. 67-68)

The sacrificer's wife sits to the south-west of the Gārhapatya fire and faces north-east. The participation of the sacrificer's wife is indispensable in an Iṣṭi as in the daily Agnihotra.

In the Pavitreṣṭi the sacralization of the sacrificer's wife is now performed. The Adhvaryu or Āgnīdhra hands over a cord made of *muñja* grass to the wife, who ties it around her waist. This may be regarded as a substitute for the man's sacred thread (*yajñopavīta*). By girdling herself with this grass cord the sacrificer's wife becomes eligible for taking part in the actual performance of the ritual.

Next, the Adhvaryu takes the vessel containing clarified butter from the Gārhapatya fire, places it in front of the sacrificer's wife, and asks her to gaze at it.

1.4.4 *Taking Up the Clarifed Butter* (Figs. 69-72)

The sacralization of the clarified butter continues with the 'taking up of the clarified butter' (*ājyagrahaṇa*). After having placed the ladles side by side on the altar, the Adhvaryu first places a small amount of clarified butter in the *juhū* ladle with a spoon called *sruva* and places it in front of him at his right and outside the altar. He similarly places a small amount of clarified butter in the *upabhṛt* and *dhruvā* ladles and places them also outside the altar. Among these three ladles, it is the first two that are generally used in performing *homa*, although the *dhruvā* is used towards the end of the ritual.

1.4.5 *Sacralization of the Fuel and the Like* (Fig. 73)

Next, the fuel sticks, altar and bundles of *darbha* grass for strewing over the altar are sacralized with holy water. The Adhvaryu sprinkles this sacralized water over the fuel sticks, altar and bundles of *darbha* grass, thereby sacralizing them.

1.4.6 *Untying and Spreading Darbha Grass Over the Altar and Arranging the Ladles* (Figs. 74-77)

The Adhvaryu loosens some of the bundles of *darbha* grass that he has just sacralized with holy water and spreads them over the altar. Next, the ladles are placed on this grass in front of and to the right of where the Adhvaryu usually sits. The vessel containing clarified butter is also placed together with the *sruva* on the grass on the altar.

1.4.7 *Arrangement of the Sacrificial Cakes* (Figs. 78-85)

The Adhvaryu goes in front of the Gārhapatya fire and pours a little clarified butter over the baked cakes with the *sruva*. Then, taking one cake at a time, he arranges the five sacrificial cakes on the altar to the left of the ladles placed side by side. He further cuts the cakes into small pieces. The preparations for offerings are now completed.

2. Main Rites

In the main rites, the oblations are offered in the sacrificial fire to various deities in the prescribed manner.

2.1 *Preliminary Oblations*

The main rite may be considered to be divided into three parts, namely, the preliminary oblations, the principal offerings (representing the main oblations), and the subsequent oblations. The preliminary oblations begin with adding fuel to the fire.

2.1.1 *Recitation of the Kindling Verses* (Figs. 86-88)

The sacrificer stands within the altar, and makes a pledge to Agni to observe his vows, the Hotṛ stands within the altar and, facing the sacrificial fire, chants the seventeen verses accompanying the kindling of the fire (*sāmidhenī*). After the end of each verse with the utterance of the syllable '*om*', the Adhvaryu places a fuel stick on the fire.

2.1.2 *Āghāra Libations* (Figs. 89-95)

After seventeen fuel sticks have been offered in the sacrificial fire in this manner to the accompaniment of the *sāmidhenī* verses, the first libation (*āghāra*) of clarified butter is made. Using the *juhū*, the Adhvaryu pours clarified butter on the northern part of the sacrificial fire. This represents an oblation to Prajāpati, the lord of creation.

The Āgnīdhra, holding the wooden sword in his left hand, touches the sticks to the south, in the centre and to the north of the hearth of the sacrificial fire with the cord of *darbha* grass with which the fuel sticks were tied. After the first libation of clarified butter, the Hotṛ performs the invocation to Agni in his role as an ancestor (*pravara*).

The Adhvaryu then places the *juhū* on the *upabhṛt* and holding both ladles with both the hands, rises from his seat in front of the sacrificial cakes and crosses from the north of the altar to the south of it. Then, facing towards the northeast, he pours a continuous stream of clarified butter from the ladles on to the sacrificial fire. After this, he makes a second invocation, reciting the names of the sacrificer's ancestors. This constitutes the second libation of clarified butter.

2.1.3 *Fore-Offerings (prayāja)* (Figs. 96-100)

The Adhvaryu puts clarified butter into the *upabhṛt* and *juhū* and, holding the former underneath the latter, moves with his left foot first towards the south of the altar. Looking towards the northeast, he then directs the Āgnīdhra to "have (the god) listen" to the ritual formula, whereupon the Āgnīdhra replies, "So be it.

May he hear us." Next, the Hotṛ recites an oblatory verse (*yājyā*), and as the word *vauṣaṭ* is uttered at the end of the verse, the Adhvaryu pours one third of the clarified butter from the *juhū* into the sacrificial fire. This is the first fore-offering. In the second fore-offering he pours half of the remaining clarified butter, and in the third fore-offering he pours all the remaining clarified butter into the fire. Then, holding the *juhū* in his left hand, he pours clarified butter from the *upabhṛt* into the *juhū*. In the fourth fore-offering, half of the clarified butter is poured from the *juhū* into the fire, and in the fifth fore-offering the rest is used. The fore-offerings thus consist of five libations of clarified butter.

These five fore-offerings are directed to five separate deities. The first is to the fuel sticks (*samidh*), the second is to *tanūnapāt narāśaṃsa*, the third is to *iā*, the fourth is to *barhis*, i.e. the sacrificial grass supposed to be the seat for the deities of the sacrifice, and the fifth is to Agni, Soma and the dual deity Agnīṣoma.

2.1.4 *Ājyabhāga Offerings* (Figs. 101-104)

Following the five fore-offerings, two oblations of clarified butter (*ājyabhāga*) are offered, first to Agni and then to Soma. The Adhvaryu first issues a direction to the Hotṛ to recite the invitatory verse (*puronuvākyā*) for Agni and then, after the recitation of the verse, he ladles clarified butter from the *dhruvā*, which generally remains placed on the altar, into the *juhū*. Next, he crosses the altar and goes to the south and directs the Hotṛ to recite the offering verse (*yājyā*) for Agni. When the word *vauṣaṭ* at the end of the verse is uttered, the Adhvaryu pours clarified butter into the northeastern part of the sacrificial fire. This constitutes the first offering of a portion of clarified butter, and it is followed by a second similar offering, for Soma, which is poured into the southeastern part of the sacrificial fire.

2.2 *Principal Offerings* (Figs. 105-109)

Next, the principal offerings (*pradhāna-homa*), representing the climax of the Pavitreṣṭi or Darśapūrṇamāsa, is performed. In the Pavitreṣṭi it is primarily the following ten deities to whom the offerings are made; but they are different from the main deities of the New Moon and the Full Moon sacrifice. According to the ritual texts, the ten main deities of the Pavitreṣṭi are as follows : Agni Pavamāna, Sarasvatī Priyā, Agni Pāvaka, Savitṛ Satyaprasava, Agni Śuci, Vāyu Niyutvat, Agni Vratapati, Viṣṇu Śipiviṣṭa, Agni Vaiśvānara, and Dadhikrāvan. The principal offerings to the ten deities are made in the prescribed manner mentioned above.

This represents the offerings to the first deity, Agni Pavamāna and it is followed by nine similar offerings to the other deities. This method of making offerings appears not only in the principal offerings, but is also found in the two sets of offerings that precede and follow it, namely, the offering of the portions of clarified butter and the *sviṣṭakṛt* offerings and the names of the ten deities are also recited during these two latter offerings. As regards the oblations of the principal offerings, clarified butter is used for the five odd-numbered deities while pieces from each of the five sacrificial cakes are used for the five even-numbered deities.

2.3 *Subsequent Offerings*

After the principal offerings, the subsequent offerings form the concluding part of the sacrifice.

2.3.1 *Upahoma Libations* (Figs. 110-111)

After the principal offerings, the *upahoma* or the supplementary *homa* is performed. Sitting down on one knee to the north of the altar near the sacrificial fire, the Adhvaryu pours the clarified butter with which he has filled the *sruva* onto the sacrificial fire, and makes various subsequent oblations (*upahoma*) to deities such as Pavamāna, Rāṣṭrabhṛt and so on. These *homas* are peculiar to the Pavitreṣṭi.

2.3.2 *Sviṣṭakṛt Offerings* (Figs. 112-113)

As an oblation for Sviṣṭakṛt Agni, the Adhvaryu takes a small portion from clarified butter and cakes and, after the recitation of the invitatory and oblatory verses, offers them into the northeastern part of the sacrificial fire. The wooden stirring stick (*mekṣaṇa*) that was used during the preparation of the sacrificial cakes is also put on the sacrificial fire.

2.3.3 *Invocation of Iḍā* (Figs. 114-120)

The Adhvaryu places the gourd-shaped vessels for the *iḍā* in front of the sacrificial cakes and then places in front of it the *prāśitra* vessel. First, the Adhvaryu places pieces of the sacrificial cakes "about the size of the fruit of the *aśvattha* tree," in the *prāśitra* vessel. He then cuts a piece of the sacrificial cake for the sacrificer and places it to the east of the *dhruvā*. Next, he places clarified butter and pieces of sacrificial cake in the *iḍā* vessels and hands it over to the Hotṛ who holds it up in both the hands, whereupon the Adhvaryu, the Āgnīdhra, the Brahman and the sacrificer gather around him and touch the *iḍā* vessel with cords of *darbha* grass. The Hotṛ then invokes Iḍā. The Adhvaryu now issues a direction for the sacrificial cake in the *prāśitra* vessel to be taken to the Brahman, who partakes of it as his portion. The sacrificer and the other priests then partake of their respective shares.

2.3.4 *Fees for the Priests* (Figs. 121-122)

The Adhvaryu takes the rice (*anvāhārya*) that has been placed on the southern fire, places it within the altar, and recites a mantra. The sacrificer then presents it to the priests as the fees (*dakṣiṇā*) for their performance of the ritual.

2.3.5 *After-Offerings* (Figs. 123-130)

Now the after-offerings (*anuyāja*) are performed. The principal *homa* (*pradhāna-homa*) is, thus preceded by fore-offerings and followed by after-offerings.

First, the Adhvaryu directs the Āgnīdhra to place the fuel sticks for the after-offerings on the sacrificial fire. Then, using the *juhū* and *upabhṛt* ladles, he pours clarified butter on the sacrificial fire standing towards the south.

Next, the Hotṛ recites the *sūktavāka* verse while the Adhvaryu wipes the bowls of the ladles with *darbha* grass which he then throws on the sacrificial fire. This act indicates that the process of concluding the sacrifice has begun.

The Hotṛ recites the *śaṃyuvāka* verse, while the Adhvaryu throws into the sacrificial fire the three enclosing sticks that had been placed around it. As a result the frame by which the sacrificial fire had been set apart from everything else disappears.

2.3.6 *Offerings to the Consorts of the Gods* (Figs. 131-135)

The priests and the sacrificer's wife move to the vicinity of the Gārhapatya fire, where they perform 'offerings to the consorts [of the gods]' (*patnīsaṃyāja*). In spite of the name being 'offerings to the consorts (of the gods)', the offerings are made to Soma, Tvaṣṭṛ, the consorts of the gods and Agni Gṛhapati.

First the Adhvaryu, putting his right knee on the ground, and his left knee raised, pours clarified butter on the Gārhapatya fire. Then the sacrificer's wife touches him with a blade of *darbha* grass, whereupon he directs the Hotṛ to recite the invitatory verses for Soma, Tvaṣṭṛ etc. After the Hotṛ has recited the oblatory verses, the Adhvaryu again pours clarified butter into the Gārhapatya fire. The procedure is the same as that for the preliminary offerings.

According to the ritual manuals, following these offerings, the Hotṛ and the other priests can leave the ritual site.

3. Concluding Rites

3.1 *Samiṣṭayajus Offerings* (Figs. 136-137)

After offering the *patnīsaṃyāja* offerings in the Gārhapatya fire, the Adhvaryu comes back to the Āhavanīya fire, and offers the concluding offering called *samiṣṭayajus.*

3.2 *Disposal of the Holy Water* (Fig. 138)

The Adhvaryu then disposes of the remaining *praṇītā* water by pouring it onto the *darbha* grass on the altar.

The Adhvaryu returns to the sacrificial fire and makes an oblation into the sacrificial fire with the *dhruvā,* the ladle that has until now remained almost unused. When this oblation has been completed, the sacrificer partakes of a portion of sacrificial cake.

3.3 *Strides of Viṣṇu* (Fig. 139)

Starting from the 'buttocks' on the south of the altar and taking care not to go beyond the sacrificial fire, the sacrificer takes three steps towards the 'shoulder' of the altar, reciting mantras at the same time. This is based on the tradition according to which Viṣṇu regained sovereignty over the three worlds by taking three strides (*viṣṇukrama*).

The Pavitreṣṭi has now been concluded, and the priests leave the ritual site with a clockwise circumambulation.

3.4 *Relinquishing the Vow* (Fig. 140)

The sacrificer then sits near the Āhavanīya fire, prays to it silently and then reciting a mantra, relinquishes the vow.

Concluding Remarks

Like all other primitive forms of ritual, the Vedic ritual also shows a journey from the 'profane' to the 'sacred'. Everything that is used in this ritual is basically mundane (*laukika*) and is transformed into the supermundane one (*alaukika*). Thus, with the recitation of the mantras and related rites, everything situated on the sacrificial place is magically charged. The sacrificial ground and the hearths are purified. The sacrificial fire is produced on the purified place, the utensils are also purified. The sacrificer enters the domain of the sacred and formally selects the priests--all this becomes the part of the sacred. The performance is no longer a 'physical reality'. Instead, it is a meta-world.

The *homa*-ritual forms a part of other Asian religions also. One may find similarities in the *homa*-ritual of Nepal, Tibet, Japan, Indonesia and other countries where the aborigional religions were much influenced by Indian religions, especially Buddhist and Hindu. Although the early or the Theravāda Buddhism does not prescribe any *homa*-ritual, the *homa* and many other rituals play an important role in the later Tantric Buddhism which is a part of Mahāyāna. The goal of Tantric Buddhism is liberation, Nirvāṇa, but it is considerably different from the Nirvāṇa of the Theravadins. The goal of Vedic ritual is the heaven, the best possible state which the Vedic man aspires for. The sacred in the Pravitreṣṭi, is unrelated to the spiritual well-being (*niḥśreyasa*) or the spiritual salvation of the individual. The sacred in the *homa* of Tantric Buddhism closely connected with the spiritual well-being of the officiant of the rite or that of his client. In Tantric Buddhism *homa* is considered to have two aspects, namely, a spiritual aspect in which mental afflictions (*kleśa)* are mentally consumed by fire (referred to as 'internal fire') and a ritual aspect incorporating traditions going back to Vedic ritual that involve the external *homa*-offerings. A detailed survey of the *homa*-rituals would be a subject of a separate study.

The foregoing description of the Pavitreṣṭi evinces that the ancient *homa*-ritual is still preserved and is being performed in India, although the social and economic conditions have changed drastically. The spirit of the Vedic man behind such performance is obviously lacking in the present-day sacrificer or the priests, for they are not aware of the psychology of the Vedic man. Nevertheless, this and other Vedic rituals are being performed, though rarely, with great fidelity. This religion represents the proto-type of the later Hinduism and yet finds a place with the modern Hinduism.

A study of Vedic ritual is expected to be useful for a comparative study of the *homa* rituals in Asian religions and it is hoped that the present work will serve that purpose to a certain extent.

Method adopted in the translation

The text of the Pavitreṣṭi has been translated here for the first time. For the translation of the mantras cited in the text, standard translations have been reprodueed from the works of well-known scholars, except the translation of the mantras from the Taittirīya Brāhmaṇa, employed in the *upahomas* in the Pavitreṣṭi, which have been translated by the authors themselves. The additional, necessary portions are given in the brackets for an adequate understanding of the text.

List of Figures

PART I

Priests, Utensils and Preparations

<0.1> Adhvaryu : Vedamūrti Narayan Vishnu Bhanose

Fig. 1

The priest belonging to the Yajurveda, who performs most of the acts in the sacrifice and gives directions to other priests.

<0.2> Āgnīdhra : Vedamūrti Laxmikant Dixit

Fig. 2

The priest belonging to the group of the Brahman, who enkindles the sacrificial fire.

<0.3> Hotṛ : Vedamūrti Popatrao Joshi

Fig. 3

The priest belonging to the Rgveda, who invokes the deities, with mantras.

<0.4> Brahman : Vedamūrti Ekanathshastri Garge

Fig. 4

The priest who acts as the superintendent of the sacrifice.

<0.5> Sadasya : Vedamūrti Shambhushastri Ware

Fig. 5

Sadasya is a member-priest who has no particular duties.

<0.6> Sadasya : Dr. Vidyadharshastri Bhide

Fig. 6

Sadasya is a member-priest who has no particular duties.

<0.7> Yajamāna : Āhitāgni Balkrishna Hari Ambekar, with his wife and son

Fig. 7

The sacrificer and his wife have some particular duties in the performance.

The son shown in this picture has no role in the actual performance.

<0.8> Sadasya : Chintamani Balkrishna Ambekar

Fig. 8

Sadasya and his younger brother.

<0.9> The sacrificial hall and the sacred fires

Fig. 9

The sacrificial hall belongs to the Vaidika Saṃśodhana Maṇḍala, Pune, where the performance of the sacrifice took place.

<0.10> A plan of the fire-places

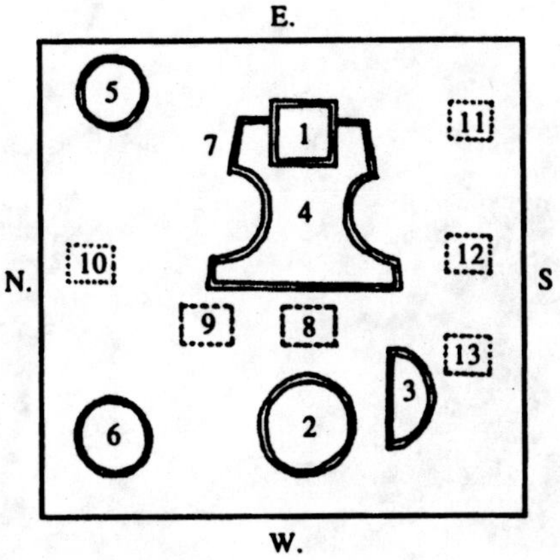

The sacrificial place

1. Āhavanīya fire
2. Gārhapatya fire
3. Dakṣiṇa fire
4. Vedi (altar)
5. Sabhya fire
6. Āvasathya fire
7. Praṇītā waters
8. The basic position of Adhvaryu priest
9. The basic position of Āgnīdhra priest
10. The basic position of Hotṛ priest
11. The basic position of Brahman priest
12. The basic position of the sacrificer
13. The basic position of the wife of the sacrificer

Fig. 10

Generally there are three sacred fires in a Śrauta performance, namely, Āhavanīya, Gārhapatya and Dakṣiṇāgni (Anvāhāryapacana). In this particular performance, two more sacred fires, namely, Sabhya and Āvasathya have been included. Kaṇe, II.2.989

<0.11> A ball of cow-dung *(gomaya-piṇḍa)*

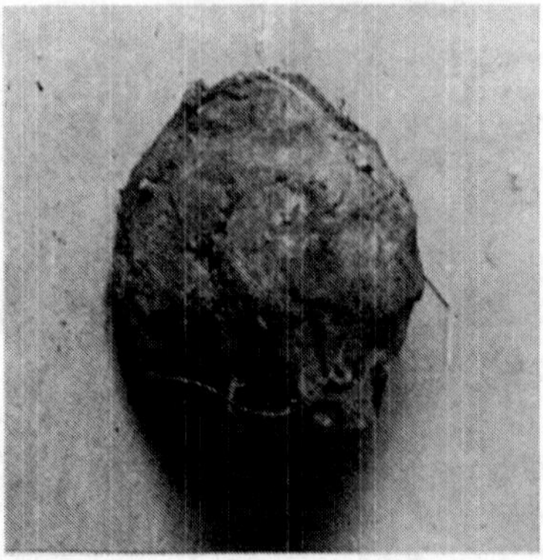

Fig. 11

Cow-dung is used as fuel.

<0.12>
A bunch of *darbha* grass

Fig. 12

The *darbha*-blades are to be used as "strainers".

<0.13> Utensils (1)

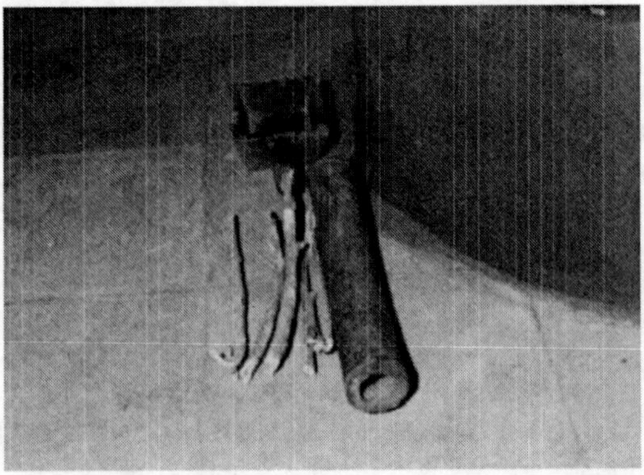

Fig. 13

Utensils (1)

<0.14> Utensils (2)

Fig. 14

The Utensils have been arranged between the Sabhya fire and the Āvasathya fire. In the following three figures (Figs. 15-17) one can see each utensil clearly.
(KŚS. ii.3.6, KID. p.7, Kaṇe, II.2.p.1020, SK. I.1.253)

<0.15> Utensils (3)

Fig. 15

The utensils (from the right) *pūrṇapātra, samidh, idhma, ṣaḍavatta.*

<0.16> Utensils (4)

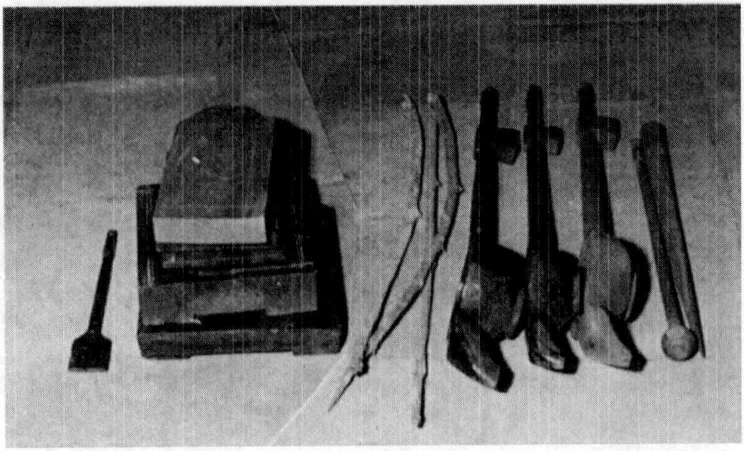

Fig. 16

The utensils (from the right) : *abhri, sruva, juhū, upabhṛt, dhruvā, paridhi, puroḍāśapātrī, araṇī, upaveṣa.*

<0.17> Utensils (5)

Fig. 17

The utensils (from the right) : *śūrpa, agnihotrahavaṇī, kapāla, kṛṣṇājina, dṛṣadupale, kuśamuṣṭi, iḍāpātrī, mekṣaṇa.*

<0.18> Utensils (6) [Nos. 1-8]

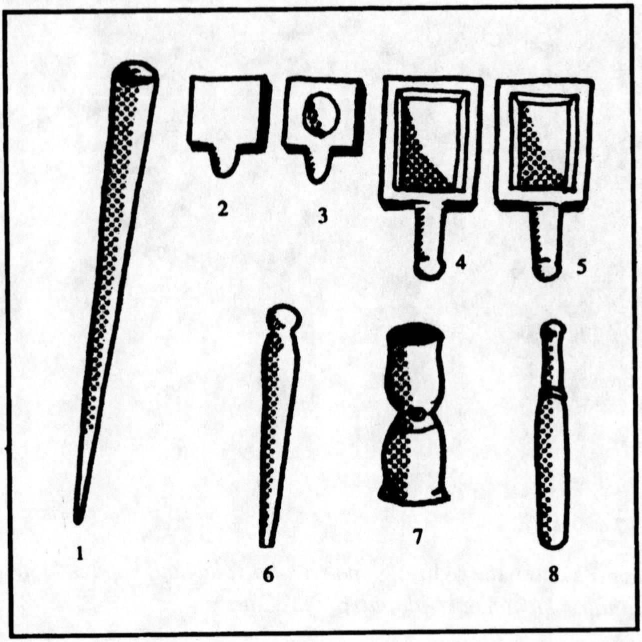

Fig. 18

The utensils are (from the left) : *abhri, puroḍāśapātrī, praṇītā, musala, ulūkhala, śamyā.*

<0.19> Utensils (7) [Nos. 9-11]

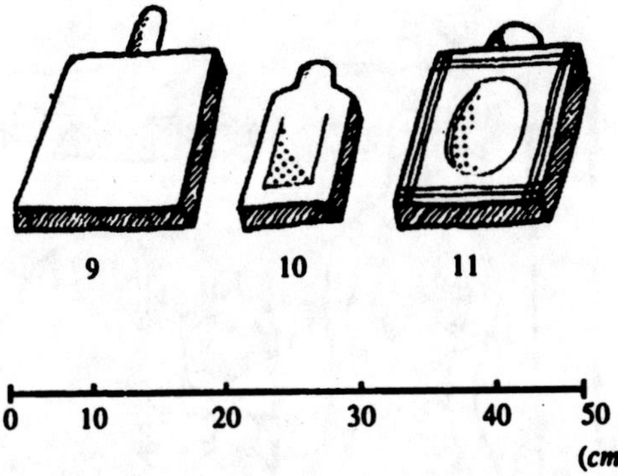

Fig. 19

The utensils are (from the left) : *puroḍāśapātrī, prāśitraharaṇa, hotṛṣadana.*

<0.20> Utensils (8) [Nos. 12-17]

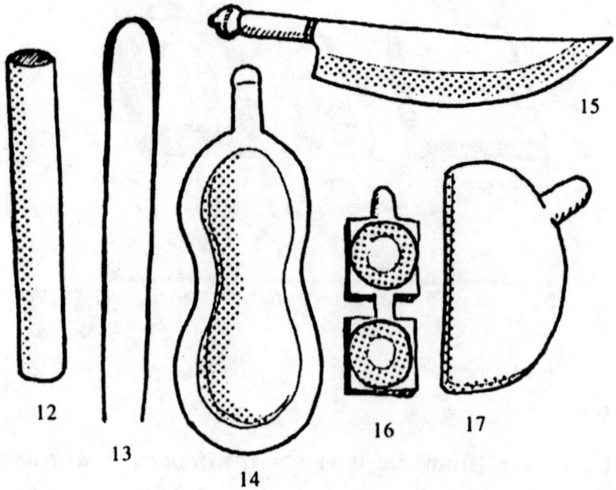

Fig. 20

The utensils are (from the left) : *dhamanī, sandaṃśa, iḍāpātrī, sphya, ṣaḍavatta, antardhānakaṭa.*

<0.21> Utensils (9) [Nos. 18-23]

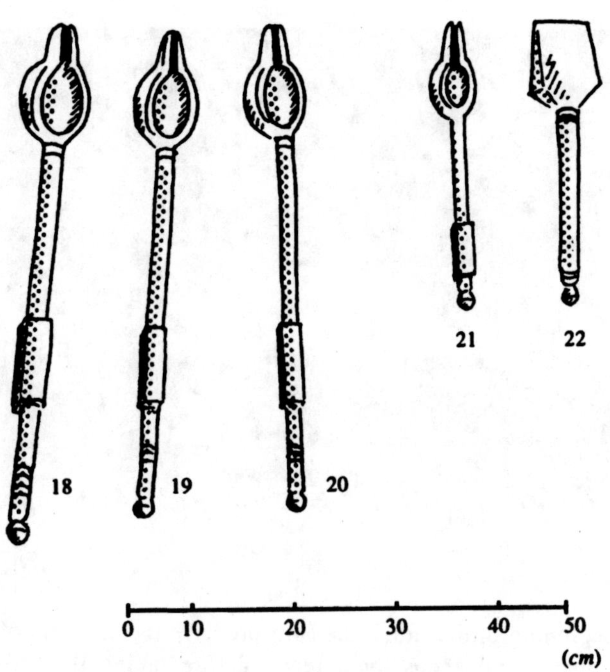

Fig. 21

The utensils (from the left) : *juhū, upabhṛt, dhruvā, prokṣaṇī, upaveṣa, sruva.* ŚK. I.1; p.253

<0.22> Preparing a *pavitra* out of *darbha* blades

Fig. 22 [7:25]

At the beginning of the ritual, the Hotṛ prepares the strainers of two *darbha* blades and keeps them ready before taking the oblation material (*havirnirvāpa*). Since the *darbha* blades are already cut, he selects from them two of equal size and of unbroken tips and consecrates them reciting a mantra.

According to KID. p.10, however, it is the Adhvaryu who prepares them after the *havirnirvāpa*. He selects two appropriate *darbha* blades and cuts them with other *darbha* blades using them as a knife. He cuts them reciting a mantra.

<0.23> Decorating the fire-places (*raṅgāvalī*)

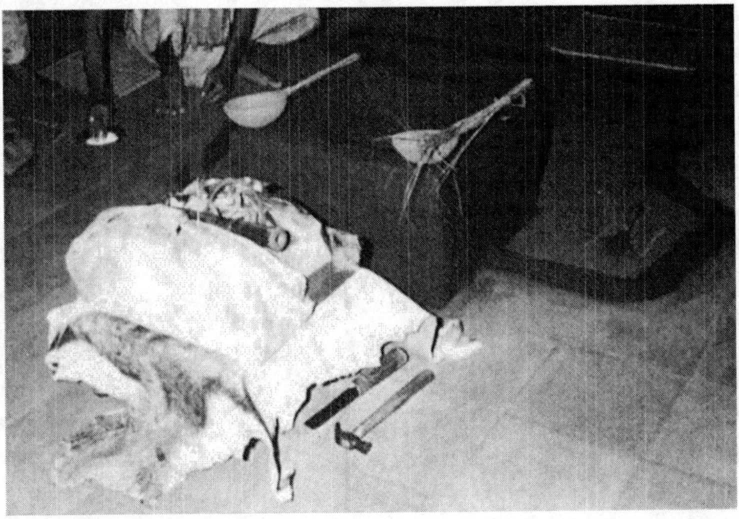

Fig. 23

The priests have placed near the fire the things necessary to churn out the fire, such as the fire-producing wooden blocks (*araṇī*), the rope and the like. ŚK I.1.30; Kaṇe, II.2.937.
Since the priests have come to the sacrificial hall from other place (i.e., Nasik), they have brought along the fire-producing wooden blocks (*araṇī*) wrapped in black antelope skin.

<0.24> Arranging the fire-producing wooden blocks (*araṇī*) (1)

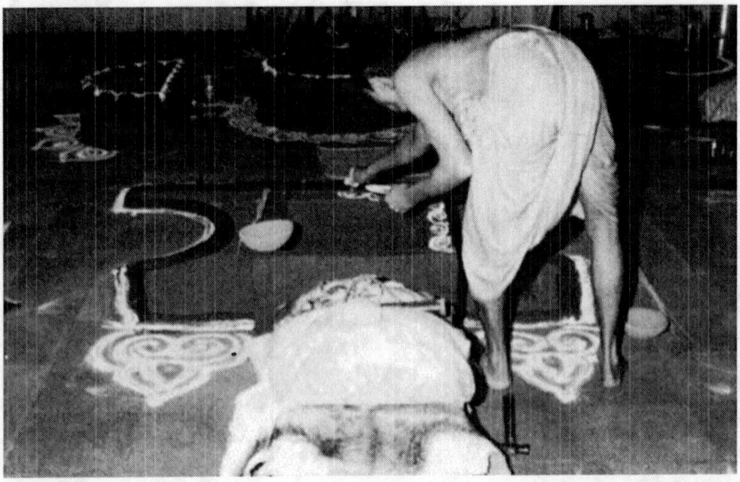

Fig. 24 [7:30]

The fire-places are being decorated with *raṅgoḷī*, i.e. powder of a particular stone, and some colours mixed in it. But this is not a *śrauta* rite. This is a *laukika* practice.
The earthen bowl placed on the Āhavanīya fire is used to carry forth the fire to other fire-places.

<0.25> Arranging the fire-producing wooden blocks (*araṇī*) (2)

Fig. 25 [7:36]

Since the sacrificer has come from some other place to perform the sacrifice, he is going to perform the rite of churning out the fire. The photo shows the things necessary to churn out the fire, such as the fire-producing wooden blocks (*araṇī*), the rope and the like.

PART II

Preliminary Rites

<1.0> Declaration of performance and purpose (*saṅkalpa*)

Fig. 26 [7:40]

The sacrificer declares his intention to perform the Pavitreṣṭi. [PIP. 2B.3]
The Adhvaryu is giving the necessary instructions to the sacrificer. The sacrificer declares his intention to perform the sacrifice, following the instructions of the Adhvaryu. He declares therein the names of the deities also, together with the names of the respective oblations. KID. 2; PIP. 2A.4 to 2B.3.

<1.1> Vitalization of the fire

<1.1.1> Vitalization of the fire (1)

Fig. 27 [7:45]

Then the priests arrange the fire-producing wooden blocks to churn out the fire. The priest places the lower kindling wood with the notch (*śamyā*) turned towards the west and while reciting the *daśahotṛ* formulas, he places the upper kindling wood, i.e. the peg cut out from it, upon the lower kindling wood. ŚK. I.1.32.

An Agnihotrin always keeps the fire alive in his house and uses it when he performs the New-moon and the Full-moon sacrifice. Symbolically he has carried that fire in those fire-producing wooden blocks from his home-town to Pune; and hence at Pune they have to churn it out.

<1.1.1> Vitalization of the fire (2)

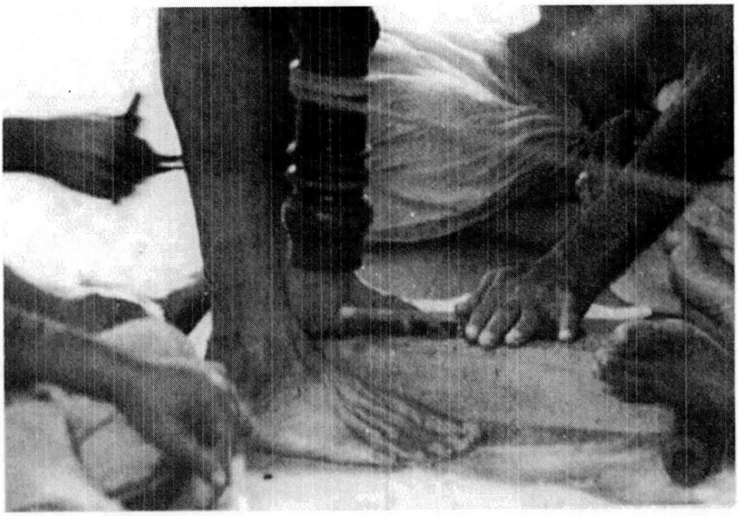

Fig. 28 [7:45]

One priest is holding the peg and the others are churning with the rope tied to it.
At the beginning and also at the end, the sacrificer churns for a while.

<1.1.1> Vitalization of the fire (3)

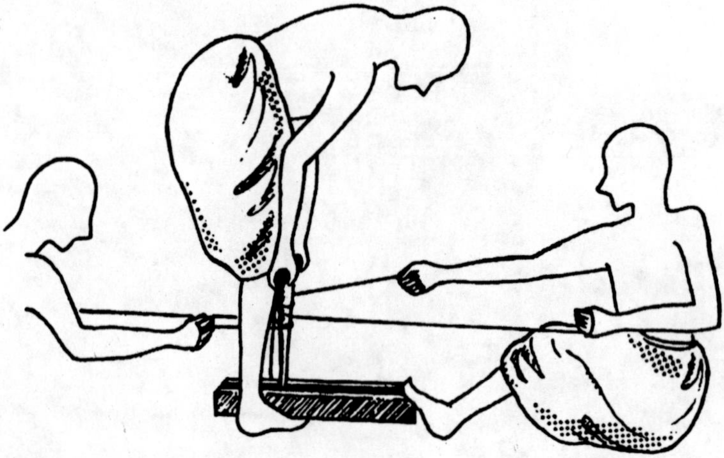

Fig. 29 [7:55]

These blocks are made of *Aśvattha* tree, which is impregnated by a *Śamī* tree, (that is, which grows upon a *Śamī* tree or which grows touching a *Śamī* tree very closely.) KŚS. iv.7.20; ŚK. I.1.5.

<1.1.2> Adding fuel to the fires (*anvādhāna*)

Fig. 30 [8:20]

The Adhvaryu adds two fire sticks each to the sacred fires. To the Āhavanīya he adds the first, reciting *mamāgne varcaḥ* --- and the second without recitation. In the same way he adds two fire sticks each to the Gārhapatya fire and to the Dakṣiṇa fire. KŚS. ii.1.3-5; KID. 3.2-8; ŚK. I.1.225.
The Adhvaryu is going to add fuel to the Gārhapatya fire.

<1.1.3> Selecting the Brahman priest (*brahmavaraṇa*)

Fig. 31 [8:27]

The sacrificer formally selects the Brahman priest. They sit near the northern buttock of the altar. The Brahman is facing towards the east, the sacrificer towards the north. The sacrificer takes gold and rice seeds in his hands and while touching the knee of the Brahman, says, "I am going to perform the Pavitreṣṭi and for that I choose you as the Brahman priest." KŚS. ii.1.17 to ii.2.1; KID. 4-5; ŚK. I.1.261.

After having been thus chosen the Brahman priest sits on his seat spread to the south of the Āhavanīya fire. His role in the ritual is mainly to supervise the performance and to see that the priests perform their acts without any flaw.

The Brahman priest has joined his hands and the sacrificer is touching the knee of the Brahman priest.

<1.1.4> Strewing the *darbha* blades

Fig. 32 [8:30]

While strewing the *darbha* blades around the fires, the Adhvaryu first places the grass to the east of the Āhavanīya fire with ends of the blades towards the north, then to the south with the ends towards the east, to the west with ends towards the north and then to the north with the ends towards the east. KŚS. ii.3.6, 7; KID. 7.6-9; ŚK. I.1.261.

No *darbha* blades are strewn with the ends towards the south. It is supposed to be the region of ancestors. Whenever there is a reference to the acts to be done around or on all sides, such as *paryagnikaraṇa, paristaraṇa,* etc., they are to be done from left to right. Regarding the rites for the ancestors, however, it is the opposite. KŚS. i.7.25,26.

The Adhvaryu who is holding the *darbha* blades is about to strew them around the Āhavanīya fire.

<1.1.5> Pāvamānī offerings

Fig. 33 [8:31]

Then the Adhvaryu makes the clarified butter hot on the Āhavanīya, cleanses the ladle and the spoon with *darbha* blades. Then he takes four spoonfuls of butter in the ladle, goes near the Āhavanīya fire and offers the oblation. He offers three oblations in this way. Since these are *svāhā* offerings, the Adhvaryu is offering them while sitting. KŚS. i.2.7.

<1.1.6> Arranging utensils (*pātrāsādana*)

Fig. 34 [8:33]

Then the Adhvaryu or the sacrificer arranges the utensils. ŚK. I.1.262; KŚS. ii.3.6,7.

Here the Adhvaryu is arranging the utensils while consecrating them.

<1.2> Fetching the holy water (*praṇītāpraṇayana*)

Fig. 35 [8:39]

The water necessary for the sacrifice is being carried (*praṇītā*) and put inside the *vedi.* Since this water is carried forth, it is called *praṇītā* water. When the Adhvaryu carries the water, he recites the mantra "*Om* you are the accomplished one (*bhūta*). I make you accomplished." KŚS. ii.3.1.

The rectangular *praṇītā* pot is seen to the north of the Āhavanīya fire.

<1.3> Preparation of the sacrificial cakes

<1.3.1a> Measuring the oblation material (*havirnirvāpa*)

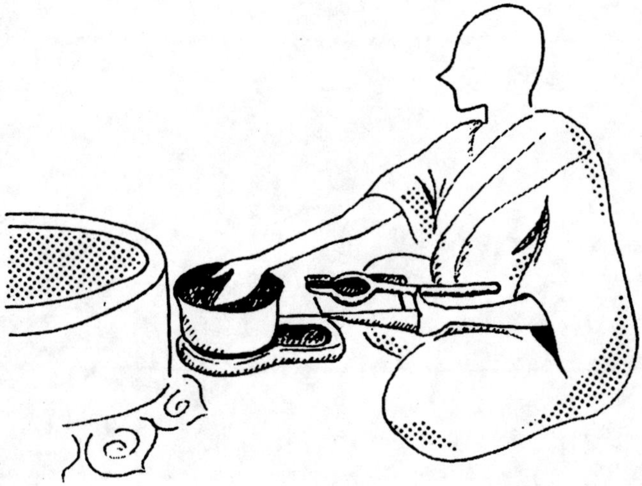

Fig. 36 [8:41]

Since the preparatory rites have been accomplished, the priests are going to make the sacrificial cakes. A priest puts the pot of grains to the west of the Gārhapatya fire. He puts tow *darbha-* strainers in the *agnihotrahavaṇī* and takes the grains in that ladle, keeping it in the winnowing basket. KŚS. ii.3.28, 29; KID. pp. 8-10; ŚK. I.1.271-72.

KŚS. states that the grains are taken from a cart placed near the sacrificial hall, but KID. which is a practical manual (prayoga) states that the grains are taken from a pot.

In this particular performance the flour was taken as the oblation material instead of grains.

<1.3.1b> Carrying the oblation material to the north of the Gārhapatya fire

Fig. 37 [8:42]

According to KŚS. the Adhvaryu takes the winnowing basket with the pot of oblation-material in it, goes to the north of the Gārhapatya fire and puts it to the west of it. KŚS. ii.3.27; KID. 10; ŚK. I.1.272

Here, however, the Adhvaryu is seen carrying the oblation-material to the place where the utensils are arranged. After the consecration, he carried it back to the west of the Gārhapatya fire.

<1.3.2> Sacralization of the water (*prokṣaṇīsaṃskāra*) (1)

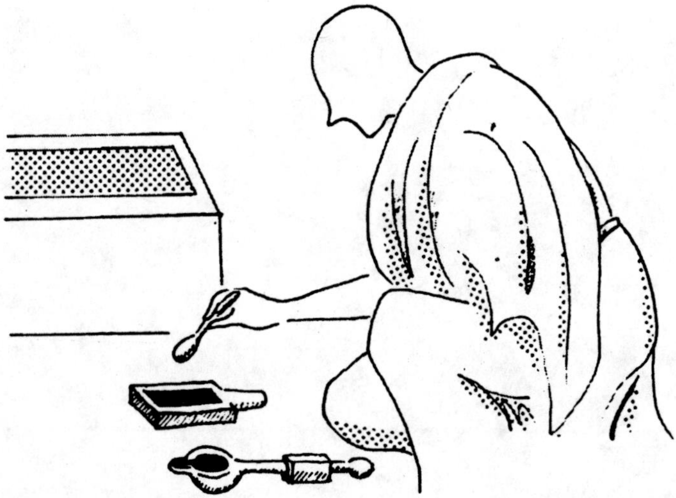

Fig. 38 [8:42]

The priest takes the waters from the *praṇītā*-cup into the *agnihotrahavaṇī* for the consecration of the pots and the oblations etc. KŚS. ii.3.32; KID. 11; ŚK. I.1.272.
The water should be consecrated first. Then only other objects can be consecrated and purified by it.
The priest is using a small wooden spoon to take the waters from the *praṇītā* cup.

<1.3.2> Sacralization of the water (*prokṣaṇīsaṃskāra*) (2)

Fig. 39 [8:42]

After taking the waters in the *agnihotrahavaṇī*, the Adhvaryu stirs it with two *darbha* blades for purification and keeps the *darbha* blades in it. Then he puts his right palm on the *agnihotrahavaṇī* which is in the left hand and gives a swing to that water (*apaḥ udiṅganam*). KŚS. ii.3.34; KID. 11; ŚK. I.1.272.

<1.3.2> Sacralization of the water (*prokṣaṇīsaṃskāra*) (3)

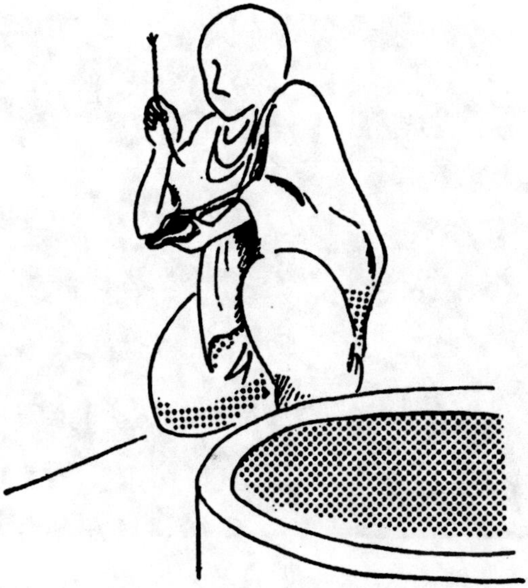

Fig. 40 [8:43]

Having taken the *darbha* blades from the *agnihotrahavaṇī,* the priest besprinkles the water in the ladle itself. KŚS. ii.3.35; KID. 11; ŚK. I.1.272.

The priest is seen here besprinkling the water in the ladle with the water in the ladle itself. According to KID. (p. 11), however, he does it with the water from the *praṇītā*-cup and with his own hand.

<1.3.3a> Sacralization of the oblation material (*haviḥprokṣaṇa*)

Fig. 41 [8:45]

He dips the *darbha* blades in the *agnihotrahavaṇī* and sprinkles that water on the oblation material and thus ritually purifies it.

<1.3.3b> Sacralization of the utensils (*pātraprokṣaṇa*)

Fig. 42 [8:46]

In the same way, the Adhvaryu sprinkles the *praṇītā* water taken from the *agnihotrahavaṇī* on the sacrificial utensils and consecrates them. KŚS. ii.3.38; KID. 11; ŚK. I.1.272.

The Adhvaryu is using the *darbha* blades to sprinkle the *praṇītā* water on the utensils. The *darbha* blades having been dipped into the water, hold some water.

<1.3.4> Making the Sacrificial Cakes

<1.3.4a> Pounding the oblation material (*haviḥkaṇḍana*) (1)

Fig. 43 [8:49]

The Adhvaryu spreads the black antelope skin and puts a miniature *ulūkhala* on it, pours some flour in it and with the miniature *musala,* symbolically pounds the oblation material to husk it. KŚS. ii.4.1 to ii.4.15; KID. 12 to 14; ŚK. I.1.283-84.

Whenever there is a reference to the spreading of the animal-skin it is spread with the hairy side up and the neck towards the east. KŚS. i.10.4. According to KŚS. ii.4.13, 14, it is the Āgnīdhra or the wife of the sacrificer who pounds the oblation material but in the photo it is the Adhvaryu who does it.

<1.3.4a> Pounding the oblation material (*haviḥkaṇḍana*) (2)

Fig. 44 [8:49]

Having placed the mortar on the black antelope skin and poured the grains into it from the winnowing basket, the Adhvaryu takes the pestle in his hand with the mantra "A mighty stone art thou formed out of timber." VS. 1.15. He puts it into the mortar with the mantra "Make ready for the deities this oblation : with careful preparation make it ready." He then himself starts pounding and calls his wife or Āgnīdhra thrice, reciting "*haviṣkṛt* come! *haviṣkṛt* come!" VS. 1.15; KID. 13.

<1.3.4b> Husking the oblation material (*nistuṣīkaraṇa*)

Fig. 45 [8:50]

It is seen that the paddy is further pounded by Āgnīdhra. He takes the winnowing basket reciting "Rain-grown art thou!" VS. 1.16, pours the pounded paddy in it with "May the rain-grown receive thee!" VS. 1.16. Then with the mantra "Cleansed off are fiends, cleansed off are the evil beings" VS. 1.16, he removes the husk from the grains. With "May Vāyu separate you," VS. 1.16, he separates the husked from the unhusked ones. He repeats these actions until all the paddy is properly husked. KID. 14.

<1.3.4c> Pulverising the grains (*taṇḍulapeṣaṇa*)

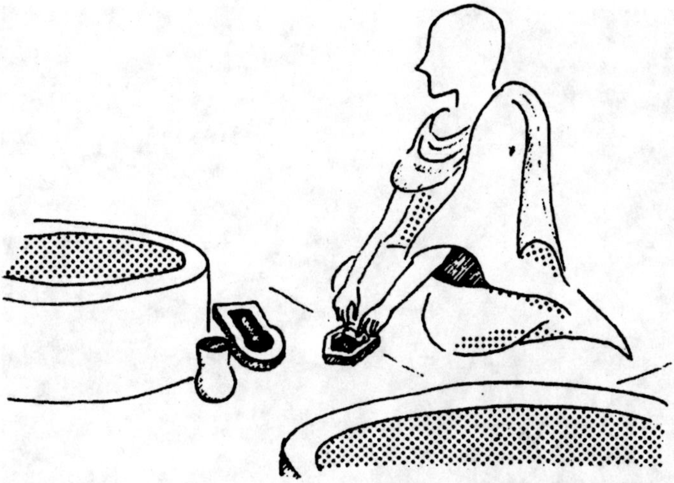

Fig. 46 [8:50]

The Adhvaryu then puts the grains on the lower crushing stone and pulverises them with the upper crushing stone. KŚS. ii.5.2-6; KID. 15,18,19; ŚK. I.1.284.

Here of course it is performed symbolically.

<1.3.4d> Shaping the sacrificial cakes (*puroḍāśakaraṇa*) (1)

Fig. 47 [8:51]

The Adhvaryu puts the strainers in a plate, takes the pulverised flour in it and sits to the west of the Gārhapatya fire. KŚS. ii.5.10,11; KID. 20; ŚK. I.1.291.

In the photo one can see the Āgnīdhra passing the strainers to the Adhvaryu.

<1.3.4d> Shaping the sacrificial cakes (*puroḍāśakaraṇa*) (2)

Fig. 48 [8:53]

The action of the Adhvaryu cannot be explained on the basis of the ritual texts. There is no reference to it. But according to the spectators who were present at the time of the performance of the Iṣṭi, the Adhvaryu poured some clarified butter in the flour taken in the *iḍāpātrī* and mixed it well with the *upaveṣa.*

<1.3.4d> Shaping the sacrificial cakes (*puroḍāśakaraṇa*) (3)

Fig. 49 [9:00]

After mixing the flour with the clarified butter, he pours the flour in the *iḍāpātrī* into the big plate with the *upaveṣa*. He then mixes all the flour well in the plate.

<1.3.4d> Shaping the sacrificial cakes (*puroḍāśakaraṇa*) (4)

Fig. 50 [9:04]

The Adhvaryu is pouring the water into the flour with the mantra "With plants let waters, plants with sap be mingled. United be the rich ones with the moving. The sweet ones and the sweet be joined together." VS. 1.121. According to the tradition, however, the Āgnīdhra pours the heated water and the Adhvaryu receives it holding two strainers on the flour in the vessel. KŚS. ii. 5.2,13; KID. 20,21; ŚK. I.1.291.

<1.3.4d> Shaping the sacrificial cakes (*puroḍāśakaraṇa*) (5)

Fig. 51 [9:04]

Then he kneads the dough with the mantra *om janayatyai tvā saṃyaumi,* i.e. "I mix you for a new birth." KŚS. ii.5.14; KID. 21.
He prepares as many balls of the dough as are required according to the number of the cakes to be offered.

<1.3.4d> Shaping the sacrificial cakes (*puroḍāśakaraṇa*) (6)

Fig. 52 [9:08]

The Adhvaryu prepares five balls of the dough, since in the Pavitreṣṭi, five cakes are to be offered to various deities.
He then flattens the balls reciting the mantra "Spread thyself widely forth, thou, widely spreading. So may the Lord of sacrifice spread widely."

<1.3.4d> Shaping the sacrificial cakes (*puroḍāśakaraṇa*) (7)

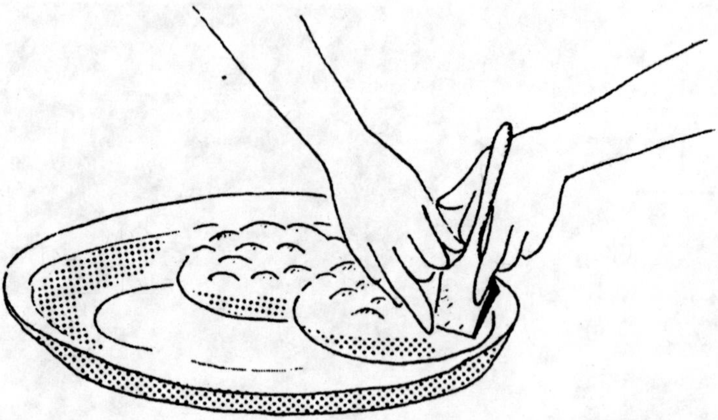

Fig. 53 [9:10]

After flattening the balls, he gives them the shape like the back of a tortoise.

This practice is borrowed from another tradition. ŚK. I.1.286.

<1.3.4d> Shaping the sacrificial cakes (*puroḍāśakaraṇa*) (8)

Fig. 54 [9:18]

In this way, he prepares five cakes as are needed for the sacrifice.

<1.3.4e> Baking the sacrificial cakes (*puroḍāśaśrapaṇa*)

Fig. 55 [9:20]

Then the Adhvaryu, with the help of the other priests, puts the five potsherds (*kapāla*) directly on the fire. Then the cakes are put on each *kapāla*.

After that, some water is smeared on each cake. Then he recites the mantra *agniṣ ṭe tvacaṃ mā hiṃsīt.....* "Thy skin let Agni harm not. In highest heaven let the God Savitar bake thee."

Actually, according to the text, the cakes are baked putting the burning embers on them, but the procedure is different here.

<1.3.4f> A break

Fig. 56 [9:27]

The priests take a small break after placing the cakes for baking.

<1.3.4g> Cooking the rice

Fig. 57 [9:28]

The wife of the sacrificer cooks rice on the fire which has been placed in a corner of the hall. This fire is not consecrated and, therefore, is called *laukika*. The rice is to be served to the priests afterwards as sacrificial fees.
According to KŚS. ii.5.27, the rice is cooked by the Adhvaryu and on the southern fire, which is a sacrificial one. ŚK. I.1.291.

<1.4> **Construction of the altar** (*vedikaraṇa*)

<1.4.1> Digging up the ground and marking out the altar (1)

Fig. 58 [9:46]

The Adhvaryu takes the wooden sword in his left hand together with the grass-blade placed formerly on the altar, touches the wooden sword with his right hand and recites the verse, "Indra's right arm art thou, sharp with a thousand spikes, a hundred edges. The keen-edged wind art thou the foeman's slayer." VS. 1.24. Before carrying the *stambayajus,* he does not touch himself or the earth with wooden sword which is sharpened by the hand symbolically.

<1.4.1> Digging up the ground and marking out the altar (2)

Fig. 59 [9:46]

While tracing the altar, the Adhvaryu draws with the wooden sword three lines on the altar. He starts from the west and ends towards the east. First he draws the southern one, then the middle one and then the northern one. ŚK. I.1.301.

<1.4.1> Digging up the ground and marking out the altar (3)

Fig. 60 [9:47]

After drawing the three lines, the Adhvaryu gives out the call to the Āgnīdhra, "Carry thrice." Then the Āgnīdhra takes off the earth from the lines drawn and throws it away on the *utkara,* with the mantra, "On this earth's farthest end, god Savitar, bind him with hundred fetters, bind the men who hate us and whom we hate. Thence do not release him." VS. 1.25.

<1.4.1> Digging up the ground and marking out the altar (4)

Fig. 61 [9:47]

After having thrown the clods of earth etc. on *utkara,* the Āgnīdhra comes back near the altar and sprinkles water on the lines drawn.

<1.4.1> Digging up the ground and marking out the altar (5)

Fig. 62 [9:47]

Having sprinkled water on the lines drawn, the Āgnīdhra is seen levelling the ground, with his hand.

<1.4.1> Digging up the ground and marking out the altar (6)

Fig. 63 [9:49]

Then the Adhvaryu digs the altar three fingers deep, with *abhri,* i.e. the wooden scraper, informing the Brahman priest saying, *brahman, pūrvaṃ parigrahaṃ parigṛhṇāmi* ("O Brahman, I will do the first tracing.") In the same manner, he does the second tracing.

<1.4.1> Digging up the ground and marking out the altar (7)

Fig. 64 [9:49]

Having done the second tracing with the permission of the Brahman, the Adhvaryu levels the ground with the wooden sword. While doing so, he makes the altar slightly prone towards the east.
The former half of the rites of preparing the altar has been accomplished.

<1.4.1> Digging up the ground and marking out the altar (8)

Fig. 65 [9:50]

The Adhvaryu then holds the *prokṣaṇī* ladle above the altar. The Āgnīdhra, who is standing nearby with the wooden sword in his hand instructs him to put down the *prokṣaṇī* water, to bring the sacrificial faggot, gird the sacrificer's wife and so on. KŚS. ii.6.25, 26.

<1.4.2> Cleansing the utensils (*pātrasammārga*)

Fig. 66 [9:53]

After heating the spoons and the ladles on the Gārhapatya fire, the Adhvaryu cleanses them by means of the tips of grass. He first cleanses from the bottom to the top and also inside the bowl and then from the bottom to the top and also the outer part of it. Then he sprinkles it with water, again heats it and gives it to the Āgnīdhra. KŚS. ii.6.39,40.

<1.4.3> Girdling the sacrificer's wife (*patnīsannahana*) (1)

Fig. 67 [9:55]

The Adhvaryu (or the Āgnīdhra) gives a three-stranded yoke-halter made of *muñja* grass to the wife of the sacrificer, who is sitting to the south-west of the Gārhapatya fire, with her face to the north-east. She ties is round her waist. KŚS. ii.7.1; KID. 31; ŚK. I. 1.313.
The girdle is considered as a substitute for the sacred thread (*yajñopavīta*). Through this rite, the wife of the sacrificer is ritualistically qualified to participate in the ritual.

<1.4.3> Girdling the sacrificer's wife (*patnīsannahana*) (2)

Fig. 68 [9:55]

The Adhvaryu takes away the pot of clarified butter from the Gārhapatya fire and makes the sacrificer's wife gaze on the clarified butter in the pot. The Adhvaryu then puts that pot within the altar to the rear of the *prokṣaṇī* pot: Thus, the clarified butter is consecrated and made ready for oblation. KŚS. ii.7.4; KID. 31; ŚK. I.1.313.

The wife of the sacrificer is holding a bunch of *darbha* grass in her hand.

<1.4.4> Taking up the clarified butter (*ājyagrahaṇa*) (1)

Fig. 69 [9:56]

The Adhvaryu looks at the clarified butter with the verse *om tejo' si......* "Light art thou, thou art splendid, thou art Amṛta." He then takes the *juhū* ladle in his left hand together with the sacrificial broom, takes the spoon in his right hand, takes the clarified butter with it and pours it into the *juhū* once with the verse, "Thou, truly, art the God's beloved station, inviolable means of holy worship." VS. 1.31, and thrice without mantra. In the photo, the *juhū* ladle is seen filled and kept aside.

<1.4.4> Taking up the clarified butter (*ājyagrahaṇa*) (2)

Fig. 70 [9:56]

Similarly in the *upabhṛt* ladle also, he pours the clarified butter once with the mantra, "Thou, truly, art the God's beloved station, inviolable means of holy worship." VS. 1.31, and seven times without any mantra. The butter thus taken eight times in the *upabhṛt* should be, however less than that taken four times in the *juhū*.

<1.4.4> Taking up the clarified butter (*ājyagrahaṇa*) (3)

Fig. 71 [9:57]

In the same way, he takes the clarified butter in the *dhruvā* ladle once with the mantra and thrice without any recitation. All the ladles when filled are kept outside the altar to the south of it. KID. 33.

<1.4.4> Taking up the clarified butter (*ājyagrahaṇa*) (4)

Fig. 72 [9:57]

Then together with the ladles, the pot of clarified butter is also put outside the altar. The Adhvaryu is seen here pouring some more clarified butter in it from another pot.

<1.4.5> Sacralization of the fuel and the like (*idhmādiprokṣaṇa*)

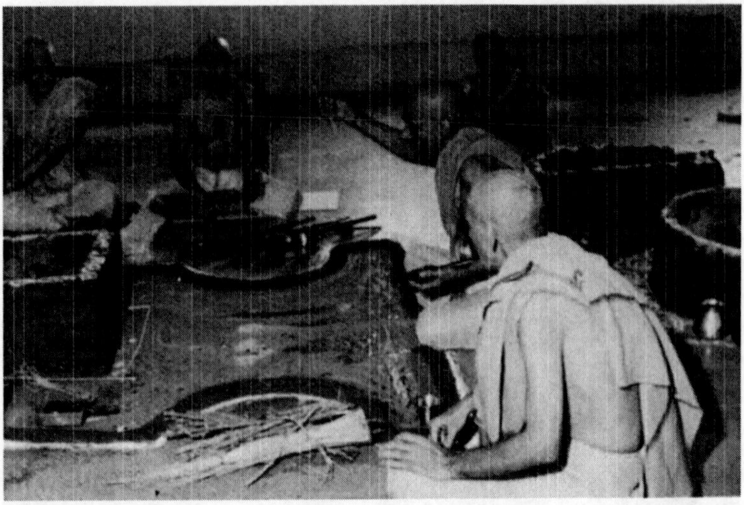

Fig. 73 [9:58]

The Adhvaryu first besprinkles the *prokṣaṇī* water with the *prokṣaṇī* water in the manner we have seen before **(Fig. 39).** Then he besprinkles the sacrificial faggot with it and then the altar. After that he puts the *barhis* i.e. sacrificial grass within the altar and besprinkles it with the *prokṣaṇī* water. He besprinkles all these things with his hand or palm upwards.

<1.4.6a> Untying bunches of *darbha* grass (*sannahanavisraṃsa*)

Fig. 74 [9:58]

The Adhvaryu unties the knot of the sacrificial grass.

<1.4.6b> Spreading the *darbha* grass (*barhirāstaraṇa*)

Fig. 75 [9:59]

Then he spreads that grass over the altar, starting from the southern shoulder of the altar and ending towards the northern shoulder of it. The grass he spreads with its tips towards the east. He performs this act reciting, "I spread thee, wool-soft, goods for gods so sit on." VS. 2.2.

<1.4.6c> Arranging the ladles (1)

Fig. 76 [10:02]

He places the ladles one by one on the sacrificial grass, in the following manner. First he touches the grass with his left hand and places the *juhū* ladle on it with the right one. Then he puts his left hand over the *juhū* with the right, takes the *upabhṛt* and places it within the altar. He then places the *dhruvā* in the same way.

<1.4.6c> Arranging the ladles (2)

Fig. 77 [10:02]

After he has put all the ladles, the Adhvaryu takes in the right hand the *ājyasthālī* and the spoon and in the left the plate for the sacrificial cakes. Then turning to his right, he comes to the west of the Gārhapatya fire to start the procedure of *puroḍāśābhighāraṇa* and *havirudvāsana*.

<1.4.7> Arrangement of the sacrificial cakes

<1.4.7a> Sprinkling the cakes with clarified butter (*puroḍāśābhighāraṇa*)

Fig. 78 [10:04]

Having come to the Gārhapatya fire the Adhvaryu sits to the west of it and puts the *puroḍāśapātrī* before him. He removes the ashes from the cakes with the sacrificial broom. Then he takes some clarified butter in the spoon from the pot and besmears first the plate with it and then the *puroḍāśa* (which is kept in the fire for baking).

<1.4.7b> Taking out the cakes (*havirudvāsana*)

Fig. 79 [10:05]

Then with the help of some wooden sticks, he takes off a sacrificial cake from the fire and puts it on the *puroḍāśapātrī* which is already besmeared.

<1.4.7c> Besmearing the *kapālas* with clarified butter (*kapālāñjana*)

Fig. 80 [10:05]

After having taken out all the cakes, he besmears all the potsherds in the fire with the mantra, "The potsherds which wise men called for the cauldron, these are in Pūṣan's guardianship. Let Indra and Vāyu set them free." TS. I.i.7.2.
He besmears them in the same order as they were kept in the fire. He repeats the mantra for each potshered. KID. 38.

<1.4.7d> Taking out the *kapālas.*

Fig. 81 [10:06]

He then takes the tongs and takes out the first potsherd. Then one by one he takes out all the potsherds.

<1.4.7e> Placing the oblations (*havirāsādana*) (1)

Fig. 82 [10:06]

The potsherds are removed now. The Adhvaryu is about to go to the Āhavanīya taking the *ājyasthālī* and the sacrificial cakes with him.

<1.4.7e> Placing the oblations (*havirāsādana*) (2)

Fig. 83 [10:09]

Taking the *veda* in the left hand, the Adhvaryu takes the *ājyasthālī* near the Āhavanīya and with "on this dear seat, with the dear hoe, be seated" VS. 2.6, he puts it on the sacrificial grass on the altar. Then he takes the *sphya* in his left hand and puts the cakes one by one one the sacrificial grass in the altar with the recitation of the same mantra. KID. 38.

<1.4.7f> Touching the cakes

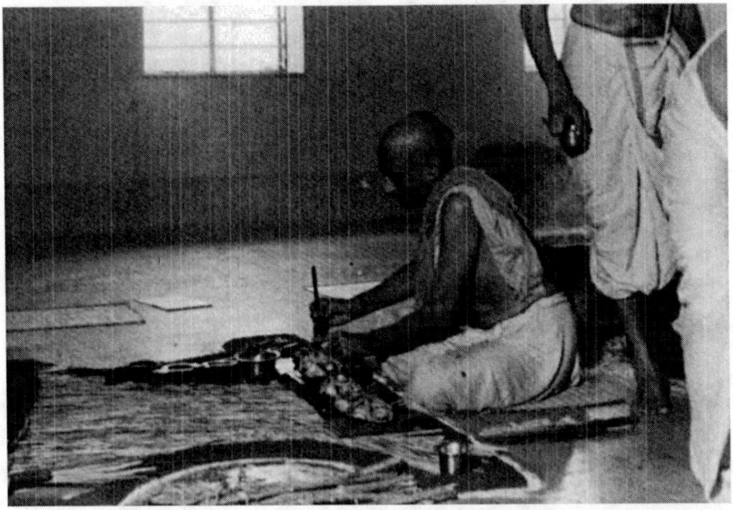

Fig. 84 [10:09]

Then the Adhvaryu first touches the clarified butter in the *ājyasthālī* with, "thou art called Dhruvā. In the law's lap they have sat down in safety. Guard these. Guard thou the sacrifice, O Viṣṇu, Keep thou the sacrifice's Lord in safety." VS. 2.6. Then with the same mantra he touches the cakes one by one and also himself and touches water after that.

<1.4.7g> Taking a vow (*vratagrahaṇa*)

Fig. 85 [10:10]

The sacrificer begins to observe the vow from this time. He optionally gets his beard, hair and nails cut. His wife also optionally gets only the nails cut. Then they eat a little food mixed with ghee. After that he takes the wooden sword, goes to the west of the Āhavanīya fire, stands facing towards the east and touching the water and while looking at the Āhavanīya fire says, "I will observe the vow, Lord of vows, Agni! May I have strength therefore. Success attend me." VS. 1.5.

PART III

Main Rites

<2.1> Preliminary oblations

<2.1.1> Recitation of the kindling verses (*sāmidhenī*) (1)

Fig. 86 [10:11]

After the Adhvaryu has spread a seat of grass for the Hotṛ to the west of the altar, and has called him, the Hotṛ enters the fire-hall to perform his duties. He sips water, stands to the west of the Āhavanīya fire facing towards the east and mutters the formula.

<2.1.1> Recitation of the kindling verses (*sāmidhenī*) (2)

Fig. 87 [10:12]

The Hotṛ then recites the seventeen *sāmidhenī* verses. At that time the Adhvaryu stands near the altar and adds a firestick to the fire, when the Hotṛ utters *om* at the end of each *sāmidhenī* verse. KID. 40.24; ŚK. 1.1.338.

<2.1.1> Recitation of the kindling verses (*sāmidhenī*) (3)

Fig. 88 [10:16]

At the end of the recitation of the verses, the Hotṛ recites the mantra *agne mahān asi brāhmaṇa bharata,* continuously. KHP. 1.2. The Adhvaryu is standing near him. After that he starts for *āghāra* libations.

<2.1.2a> The first *āghāra* libation (1)

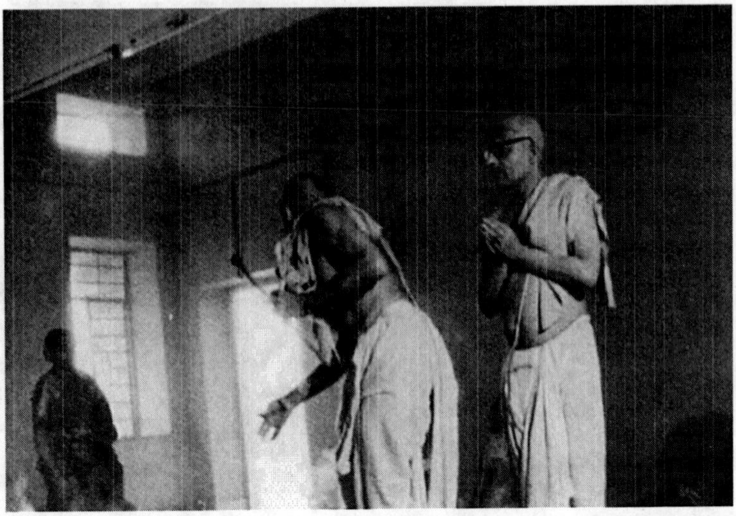

Fig. 89 [10:18]

Then the Adhvaryu takes clarified butter in a spoon, goes near the northern joint of the enclosing sticks and offers it to Prajāpati on the northern part of the fire. KID. 44.11 ff; ŚK. I.1.338.

<2.1.2a> The first *āghāra* libation (2)

Fig. 90 [10:19]

Then the Āgnīdhra, having been told by the Adhvaryu, takes the wooden sword in the left hand, goes near the southern enclosing stick and cleanses the fire place with the cord with which the sacrificial faggot was tied. KID. 45.1 ff; ŚK. I.1.338.
In the same way, afterwards, he brushes the middle and the northern enclosing sticks.

<2.1.2a> The second *āghāra* libation (1)

Fig. 91 [10:19]

Then the Adhvaryu holds the *juhū* ladle with both the hands, brings it above the *upabhṛt,* taking it from the front of the *upabhṛt* and then holding both the ladles, he gets up. KID. 46ff; ŚK. I.1.338, 339.

<2.1.2a> The second *āghāra* libation (2)

Fig. 92 [10:19]

Then, along the north of the altar, he goes to the south of the altar, first stepping out his left foot. There he stands facing towards the north-east direction. Then he pours the latter *āghāra* libation on the south-east part of the fire. He pours it towards the east without breaking the line or flow. KID. 46, 47; ŚK. I.1.339.

<2.1.2b> Duties of the Hotṛ in connection with the *sāmidhenī* libations and the *āghāra* libations (1)

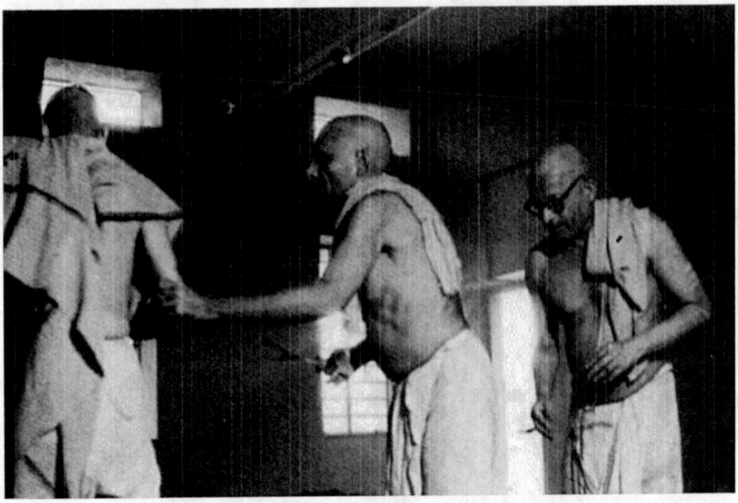

Fig. 93 [10:20]

After putting the ladles at their proper places, the Adhvaryu goes towards the north of the Āhavanīya fire with the sacrificial faggot in his hand and touches the Āgnīdhra who is standing there with the wooden sword and the cord of the sacrificial faggot in his hand. KID. 47; ŚK. I.1.339.

<2.1.2b> Duties of the Hotṛ in connection with the *sāmidhenī* libations and the *āghāra* libations (2)

Fig. 94 [10:21]

When the Hotṛ hears the words of the Adhvaryu, "I have chosen this person named N.N. as the Hotṛ of this sacrifice," he murmurs some formula and touches the right shoulder of the Adhvaryu and then that of the Āgnīdhra with his palm. Then only, the Adhvaryu takes his hand away from the Āgnīdhra. KlD. 51.

<2.1.2b> Duties of the Hotṛ in connection with the *sāmidhenī* libations and the *āghāra* libations (3)

Fig. 95 [10:22]

Then the Hotṛ with the cord by which the sacrificial faggot was tied wipes his face thrice from left to right in circumambulatory way, once reciting a formula and twice without reciting it. Then he wipes his face from right to left in the same way. KID. 52; ŚK. I.1.347.

<2.1.3> The five fore-offerings (*prayāja*) (1)

Fig. 96 [10:22]

When the Hotṛ has uttered the necessary formula, the Adhvaryu takes the clarified butter in the *upabhṛt* ladle and also in the *juhū* ladle.

<2.1.3> The five fore-offerings (*prayāja*) (2)

Fig. 97 [10:22]

Then the Adhvaryu puts that ladle over the *upabhṛt* ladle and goes to the south of the Āhavanīya fire along the north of the oblations. He steps out his left foot first. He stands there looking towards the north-east direction, and asks the Āgnīdhra to give the next necessary call. KŚS. ii.7; KID. 54; ŚK. I.1.356.

<2.1.3> The five fore-offerings (*prayāja*) (3)

Fig. 98 [10:23]

When the Hotṛ is reciting the necessary formula, the Adhvaryu should hold the ladles near his navel and after the utterance of *vauṣat,* he should offer one-third of the butter from the *juhū* ladle in the most blazing part of the fire. Then as the second *prayāja* offering, he offers the half of the remaining and then, as the third offering, all the rest from the *juhū.* KŚS. iii.3.1; KID. 54; ŚK. I.1.356.

<2.1.3> The five fore-offerings (*prayāja*) (4)

Fig. 99 [10:23]

Then the Adhvaryu holds the *juhū* in his left hand and pours in it the clarified butter from the *upabhṛt*. Then in the same way, he offers the half of it as the fourth oblation and the rest of it as the fifth oblation. KID. 56; ŚK. I.1.356.

<2.1.3> The five fore-offerings (*prayāja*) (5)

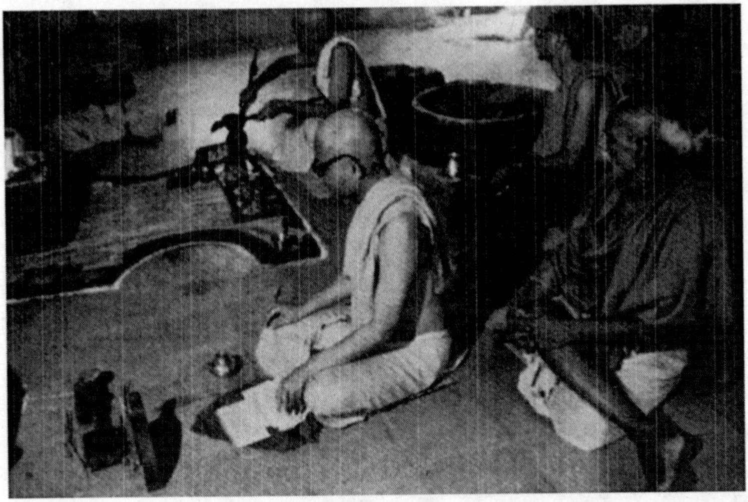

Fig. 100 [10:24]

Stepping out his right foot first, he comes back near the oblations, sits there and anoints the *dhruvā* ladle, the cakes for the deities and the *upabhṛt* accordingly, with the remnants of the clarified butter in the *juhū* ladle, KŚS. iii. 3.9; KID. 57.

<2.1.4> The first *ājyabhāga* offering (1)

Fig. 101 [10:24]

Then while still sitting, the Adhvaryu tells the Hotṛ to recite the invitatory verse to Agni. When the Hotṛ has finished, the Adhvaryu takes the clarified butter from the *dhruvā* into the *juhū*. He should take it four times, KŚS. iii.3.10; KID. 57.

<2.1.4> The first *ājyabhāga* offering (2)

Fig. 102 [10:25]

Then crossing the altar, the Adhvaryu goes to the south of the Āhavanīya fire, and gives out the call to the Hotṛ to recite the oblatory verses. KID. 62.

<2.1.4> The first *ājyabhāga* offering (3)

Fig. 103 [10:25]

When the necessary formulas are uttered, the Adhvaryu should make the offering in the eastern part of the northern half of the fire. This is the first *ājyabhāga* offering. KŚS. iii.3.20; KID. 59.
While offering he holds the ladle with its bowl turned towards the opposite side, as is seen in the photo. This practice, however, is borrowed from another tradition.

<2.1.4> The second *ājyabhāga* offering

Fig. 104 [10:29]

Then similarly the Adhvaryu goes to the south of the Āhavanīya fire and when the necessary formulas are uttered, offers the second *ājyabhāga* offering in the eastern part of the southern half of the Āhavanīya fire, holding the ladle with its bowl turned towards the opposite direction. KID. 60; ŚK. I.1.357.
KŚS. states that optionally he can offer them anywhere on the flaming fire.

<2.2> Principal offerings

<2.2.1> Offering to Agni Pavamāna (1)

Fig. 105 [10:32]

The Adhvaryu first pours some clarified butter in the *juhū,* then takes the cuttings from the cake for the deity, again pours some butter on the cake, and taking the oblation goes to the south of the Āhavanīya. KID. 60; ŚK. I.1.369.

<2.2.1> Offering to Agni Pavamāna (2)

Fig. 106 [10:33]

The Adhvaryu standing to the south of the Āhavanīya, gives order to the Āgnīdhra, *'āśrāvaya'*.
Then the Āgnīdhra utters the formula *'astu śrauṣaṭ'*. After that the Adhvaryu asks the Hotṛ priest to recite the offering verses.
In the photo, the Hotṛ is seen reciting the offering verses. The Adhvaryu is, however, not seen. KID. 61.

<2.2.1> Offering to Agni Pavamāna (3)

Fig. 107 [10:35]

After that the Adhvaryu offers the oblation to Agni Pavamāna on the fully blazing Āhavanīya fire on place between the two spots of the two *ājyabhāga* offerings.

The sacrificer sitting to the south of the Āhavanīya fire says, "This is offered to Agni Pavamāna. This is not mine."

<2.2.2> Offering to Sarasvatī Priyā (and other deities) (1)

Fig. 108 [10:38]

The Adhvaryu, then, stepping out his right foot first, comes back to the west of the Āhavanīya fire near the oblation, begins to take the oblation of clarified butter to Sarasvatī Priyā and asks the Hotṛ to recite the invitatory verses to that deity.

<2.2.2> Offering to Sarasvatī Priyā (and other deities) (2)

Fig. 109 [10:39]

Then following the same procedure he goes to the south of the Āhavanīya fire, asks the Hotṛ to recite the offering verses for Sarasvatī Priyā and at the end of it offers the oblation in the fire. The sacrificer again utters the words, "This is to Sarasvatī Priyā. This is not mine." In the same manner, the Adhvaryu offers the libations to the rest of the deities, viz., Agni Vratapati, Viṣṇu Śipiviṣṭa, Agni Vaiśvānara and Dadhikrāvan.

In the photograph, the Āgnīdhra is seen with his back to the camera.

<2.3> Subsequent offerings

<2.3.1> *Upahoma* libations (1)

Fig. 110 [10:42]

Then he sits to the north of the altar and offers the subsequent offerings (*upahoma*) taking the clarified butter from the *ājyasthālī* with the spoon. PIP. 8B.3.

<2.3.1> *Upahoma* libations (2)

Fig. 111 [10:42]

The Adhvaryu is seen with the *veda* in his left hand. He takes the clarified butter from the *ājyasthālī* and offers the oblations, one by one.

<2.3.2> *Sviṣṭakṛt* offerings (1)

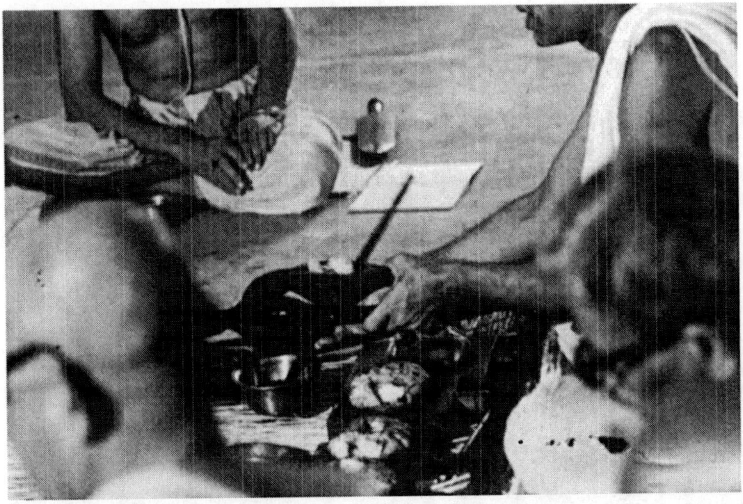

Fig. 112 [10:49]

After that the Adhvaryu first pours some clarified butter in the *juhū*. Then he takes cuttings from the northern part of the cakes, for the *sviṣṭakṛt* offering. He does not take the cuttings from the clarified butter in the *dhruvā*. He then anoints the oblation twice with the clarified butter, and goes to the south of the Āhavanīya fire. He does not anoint the parts from which he has taken the cuttings for the *sviṣṭakṛt*. PIP. 8 A. 6 to 8 B. 2; KID. 64.3 ff; ŚK. I.1.369.

According to the text of the Pavitreṣṭi he first takes the cuttings of the *sviṣṭakṛt*. After that he offers the *upahomas* and then the *sviṣṭakṛt*.

<2.3.2> *Sviṣṭakṛt* offerings (2)

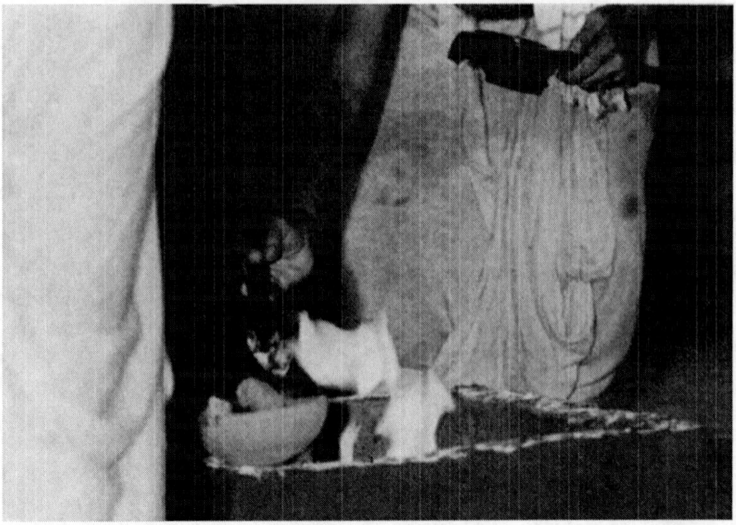

Fig. 113 [10:49]

After the recitation of the invitatory and oblatory verses, the Adhvaryu offers the *sviṣṭakṛt* offerings, on the eastern part of the northern half of the Āhavanīya fire, beyond the earlier oblations. He should offer in such a way that it does not come into contact with the previous offering. KŚS. iii.3.28; KID. 68.

<2.3.3> Invocation of Iḍā (*iḍopāhvāna*) (1)

Fig. 114 [10:50]

The Adhvaryu has the *prāśitraharaṇa* in his hand. He puts it in the altar to take in it the share of the Brahman priest.
The *anvāhārya* rice is already cooked and is seen kept on the southern fire.

<2.3.3> Invocation of Iḍā (*iḍopāhvāna*) (2)

Fig. 115 [10:50]

The Adhvaryu requests the attendant to give him a pot to be used as the *iḍā* pot.
This is done following another tradition. ŚK. I.1.372. The KŚS. and also KID. do not prescribe it.

<2.3.3> Invocation of Iḍā (*iḍopāhvāna*) (3)

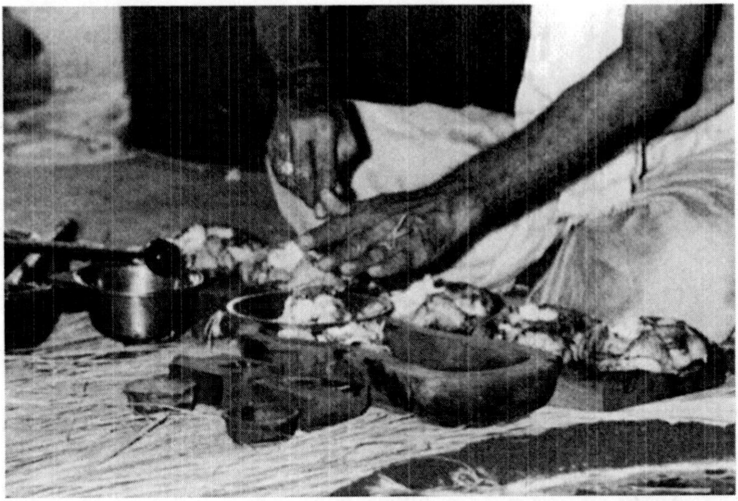

Fig. 116 [10:51]

After getting the pot, he takes a part of the cake in it for the sacrificer and puts it on the sacrificial grass next to the *dhruvā* ladle. KID. 69, 119; ŚK. I.1.382.

According to Kātyāyana's tradition the Adhvaryu first takes the portion for the Brahman and the Āgnīdhra and then that for the sacrificer. Here, however, it seems that some other tradition is followed.

<2.3.3> Invocation of Iḍā (*iḍopāhvāna*) (4)

Fig. 117 [10:52]

Then the Adhvaryu first pours some clarified butter in the *iḍā* vessel, takes the cuttings from the southern and the middle part of the cakes and anoints them again with the clarified butter. KID. 69, 113; ŚK. I.1.383.

<2.3.3> Invocation of Iḍā (*iḍopāhvāna*) (5)

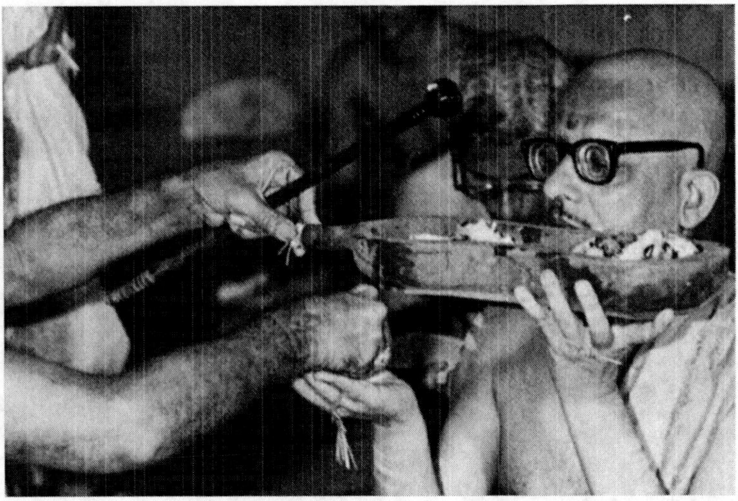

Fig. 118 [10:54]

Then the Adhvaryu faces towards the west, gives the *iḍā* pot to the Hotṛ and without leaving the contact with the *iḍā* pot goes around the Hotṛ from left to right and comes back to his place. KID. 70. ff; ŚK. I1.1.383.

<2.3.3> Invocation of Iḍā (*iḍopāhvāna*) (6)

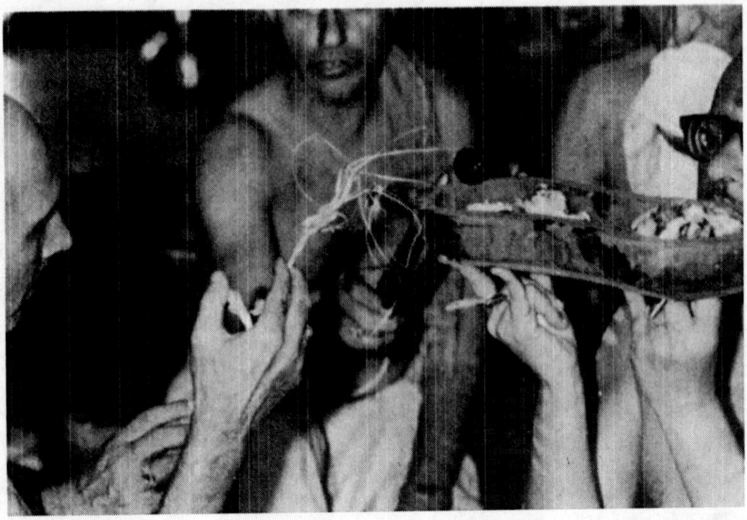

Fig. 119 [10:55]

After coming back to his place, the Adhvaryu should, facing towards the south, anoint the upper part of the Hotṛ's index finger taking the clarified butter from the *iḍā* pot itself with the spoon. KID. 70 ff; ŚK. I.1.383.

<2.3.3> Invocation of Iḍā (*iḍopāhvāna*) (7)

Fig. 120 [10:55]

The Hotṛ should wipe his lower lip with the clarified butter applied to his middle phalanx and the upper one with that applied to his upper phalanx. Then he holds the *iḍā* pot in front of his mouth and invokes it. KID. 70ff; ŚK. I.1.383.

<2.3.4> Fees for the priests (*anvāhārya*) (1)

Fig. 121 [11:00]

The Adhvaryu asks for the rice which is to be given as the sacrificial fees.

Here it seems that the procedure of some other tradition is followed. According to KŚS. and KID., the Adhvaryu should first pour clarified butter on the *anvāhārya* rice. Then he should take it towards the north, then towards the west between the Gārhapatya and the southern fires, further, along the south of the southern fire between the Brahman and the sacrificer, and along the front of the Āhavanīya fire between the *praṇītā* waters and the *utkara* and then place it within the altar. KID. 75-76; ŚK. I.1.391.

<2.3.4> Fees for the priests (*anvāhārya*) (2)

Fig. 122 [11:00]

The Adhvaryu touches the cooked rice with the mantra, *prajāpater bhāgo 'si*...KŚS. iii. 4.27. The sacrificer then announces, "I will distribute this rice equally to all the priests for the completion of the sacrifice," and gives it to each one of them.

<2.3.5> After-offerings (*anuyāja*) (1)

Fig. 123 [11:04]

The Adhvaryu gives the *anuyāja* firestick, which he has kept aside (at the time of the *sāmidhenī* offerings) to the Āgnīdhra and asks him to put it on the fire. Then he takes the clarified butter from the *upabhṛt* in the *juhū*, keeping only a little in the *upabhṛt* and in the previous manner goes to the south of the Āhavanīya fire with the two ladles.

<2.3.5> After-offerings (*anuyāja*) (2)

Fig. 124 [11:05]

The Adhvaryu gives the *sphya* to the Āgnīdhra, after he has sprinkled with the *praṇītā* water the passage for going to the south of the Āhavanīya fire. Then he gets ready for the offering, by taking the clarified butter in the *juhū*.

<2.3.5> After-offerings (*anuyāja*) (3) (*sūktavāka, 1*)

Fig. 125 [11:06]

The Adhvaryu dips the bunch of grass (*prastara*) into the ladles. The tips he dips in the *juhū,* the middle portion in the *upabhṛt* and the roots in the *dhruvā*. Then he takes out a *darbha* blade from the *prastara* (and holds the *prastara* erect in the *juhū*). KID. 81ff; ŚK. I.1.403.

<2.3.5> After-offerings (*anuyāja*) (4) (*sūktavāka, 2*)

Fig. 126 [11:08]

The Adhvaryu holds the *prastara* erect on the Āhavanīya fire, while the formulas are being recited. One *darbha* blade he takes aside from the bunch.
The method of holding the *prastara* erect on the fire seems to be taken from the Vārāha tradition. ŚK. I.1.402.

<2.3.5> After-offerings (*anuyāja*) (5) (*sūktavāka, 3*)

Fig. 127 [11:08]

The Āgnīdhra is standing to the north-west of the Āhavanīya fire with the *sphya* in his hand. The Adhvaryu offers the *prastara* in the fire.

<2.3.5> After-offerings (*anuyāja*) (6) (*sūktavāka, 4*)

Fig. 128 [11:10]

After the Adhvaryu has offered the *prastara* in the fire, the Āgnīdhra make him a request *'anuprahara'* "throw the remaining *darbha* blade in the fire." The Adhvaryu then puts on the fire the *darbha* blade set apart. KID. 85; ŚK. I.1.404.

<2.3.5> After-offerings (*anuyāja*) (7) (*śaṃyuvāka, 1*)

Fig. 129 [11:11]

When the *śaṃyuvāka* is being recited, the Adhvaryu puts the enclosing sticks on the Āhavanīya fire. KID. 86-87; ŚK. I.1.404.

<2.3.5> After-offerings (*anuyāja*) (8) (*śaṃyuvāka,* 2)

Fig. 130 [11:12]

The Adhvaryu then takes the *juhū* and the *upabhṛt*, sits to the north of the Āhavanīya fire and offers the remnants of the oblations on it from those ladles. KID. 87ff; ŚK. I.1.404.

<2.3.6> Offerings to the consorts of the gods (*patnīsaṃyāja*) (1)

Fig. 131 [11:15]

Then all the priests go the Gārhapatya fire. While going, the Adhvaryu goes between the southern and the Gārhapatya fire and sits to the south of the Gārhapatya fire facing towards the north-east, next to the sacrificer's wife. The Āgnīḍhra sits to the north of it and the Hotṛ sits between these two. Then touching the earth with the right knee and having the left knee up, the Adhvaryu offers the oblations of the clarified butter into the Gārhapatya fire. KID. 87ff.; ŚK. I.1.422.

<2.3.6> Offerings to the consorts of the gods (*patnīsaṃyāja*) (2)

Fig. 132 [11:17]

The Adhvaryu, while being touched by the wife of the sacrificer, tells the Hotṛ to recite the invitatory verses to the consorts of the gods. KID. 90; ŚK. I.1.422.
In the photograph, it is seen that she is touching the Adhvaryu with a *darbha* blade.

<2.3.6> Offerings to the consorts of the gods (*patnīsaṃyāja*) (3)

Fig. 133 [11:17]

When the Hotṛ has recited the oblatory verses, the Adhvaryu should offer clarified butter to the consorts of the gods. KID. 90-91; ŚK. I.1.422.

<2.3.6> Offerings to the consorts of the gods (*patnīsaṃyāja*) (4)

Fig. 134 [11:18]

After the offerings to Agni Gṛhapati, the Adhvaryu takes clarified butter five times in the *iḍāpātrī* and with his face towards the east gives it to the Hotṛ. Then still touching the *iḍā,* he sits before the Hotṛ facing the west, takes the *iḍā* given by the Hotṛ, takes some clarified butter from it and anoints the top and the middle phalanxes of the finger of the Hotṛ with it. Then the Adhvaryu takes the clarified butter four times from the *iḍā* and pours it into Hotṛ's hand. The fifth one the Hotṛ himself takes and holds the *iḍā* near his mouth and invokes it.

<2.3.6> Offerings to the consorts of the gods (*patnīsaṃyāja*) (5)

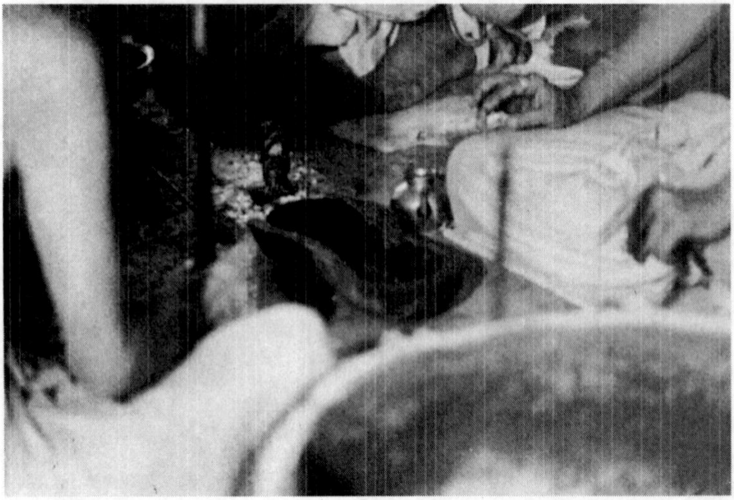

Fig. 135 [11:18]

The Hotṛ priest wipes his lower lip with the clarified butter applied to his middle phalanx and the upper one with that applied to the upper phalanx of the index-finger; and then pours water on his finger.

The water-pot with the spout is seen near the right knee of the Hotṛ priest.

PART IV

Concluding Rites

<3> Concluding Rites

<3.1> *Samiṣṭayajus* offerings (1)

Fig. 136 [11:20]

After offering the *patnīsaṃyāja* offerings the Adhvaryu is coming back to the Āhavanīya fire to offer the concluding offering called *samiṣṭayajus.* If he were to perform the *samiṣṭayajus* offerings before the *patnīsaṃyāja,* his sacrifice would be completed in the Gārhapatya fire, i.e., on the west. Hence, he offers the *samiṣṭayajus* oblations at this particular time, thinking, "Let the sacrifice be completed in the east." ŚatBr. I.ix.2.25.

<3.1> *Samiṣṭayajus* offerings (2)

Fig. 137 [11:21]

The Adhvaryu then stirs the clarified butter in the *dhruvā* ladle, takes it in the *juhū,* holds a bunch of *kuśa* grass in the left hand and offers the *samiṣṭayajus* oblation sitting near the spread grass with the mantra, "O Deities, ye knowers of the pathway, walk on the pathway having known the pathway. God, Lord of Spirit, hail! bestow upon the wind this sacrifice."
In the photo the Āgnīdhra is seen helping the Adhvaryu and stirring the clarified butter for him.

<3.2> Disposal of the holy water (*praṇītāvimokṣa*)

Fig. 138 [11:24]

The Adhvaryu takes the *praṇītā* water, goes along the front of the Āhavanīya fire to the south of it and pours that water within the altar. KID. 95-96; ŚK. I.1.422-423.

<3.3> Strides of Viṣṇu (*viṣṇukrama*)

Fig. 139 [11:26]

The sacrificer stands near the right buttock of the altar and takes three steps towards the Āhavanīya fire in the eastern direction. The first step he takes with the right foot reciting, "By Jagatī metre in the sky stood Viṣṇu. Therefrom excluded is the man who hates us and whom we detest." The left foot he puts near it. Then second step also he takes with the right foot towards the east with, "By Triṣṭup metre in the air strode Viṣṇu. Therefrom excluded is the man who hates us and whom we detest." VS. 2.25.
Then the third step he takes towards the east with "By Gāyatrī metre upon the earth strode Viṣṇu. Therefrom excluded is the man who hates us and whom we detest." He should not, however, cross the Āhavanīya fire. KID.97.

<3.4> Relinquishing the vow (*vratavisarga*)

Fig. 140 [11:31]

After praying to the Gārhapatya fire, the sacrificer sits near the altar facing towards the Āhavanīya fire, prays to it and then relinquishes the vow. KID. 99ff.; ŚK. I.1.423

APPENDIX I

Translation of the *Pavitreṣṭiprayoga*

This is an English translation of the manual of the Pavitreṣṭi following which the priests performed the sacrifice in Pune. It is a manuscript preserved in the library of the Bhandarkar Oriental Research Institute, Pune - 411 004. The number of the manuscript is No. 422 of 1983-84, New No. 1. The text is printed after the translation. The edited text is reproduced here in the roman script as Appendix No. II.

Since it is a manual of a modified form of the Iṣṭi (*vikṛtiyāga*), all the details of the ritual are not mentioned therein. We have therefore, supplied the necessary information into brackets wherever necessary. The translation of the *sāmidhenī* verses is added in full from *Hautrika*, the *Kātyāyana Hautra Pariśiṣṭa*, translated by Prof. C. G. Kashikar. The mantras accompanying the twenty Upahoma libations are from the *Taittirīya Brāhmaṇa* III.vii.12.1-6 and are translated by us for the first time. We have referred to the relevant folio-numbers of the text in square brackets and the numbers of the photographs of the corresponding ritual in round brackets.

[1B] Obeisance to Śrī Gaṇeśa. Now begins (the description of) Pavitreṣṭi. It should be performed on a *parvan* day, (i.e on the full moon day or the new moon day). It is (performed) for the destruction of all the sins. There is a verse in praise of this sacrifice. "One who performs (the rites) Vaiśvānarī, Vrātapatī, Pavitreṣṭi and the Mṛgāreṣṭi at their proper times, purifies twenty generations of his family."

Bhagavān Bodhāyana has stated, "He purifies his ten former generations, ten following generations and himself, i.e. the twenty-first and (thus) the lineage." By the repetition seen as *ṛtāv ṛtau* the obligatoriness (*nityatva*) of these rites is denoted. Also, "all acceptances of evil sacrificial fees are purified by the Pavitreṣṭi." When the Pavitreṣṭi is performed for the destruction of the sin, caused by the acceptance of (evil) sacrificial fees, the Anvārambhaṇīyā Iṣṭi should be performed, because of the optional character (of the Iṣṭi). When it is to be performed every year as an obligatory rite, the Anvārambhaṇīyā should be performed only at the time of the first performance. Since the Mitravindā and the Pavitreṣṭi are mentioned together (in the scripture) and since the Pavitreṣṭi is not described in our own Vedic recension, [2A] the one which is prescribed by Bodhāyana etc. is being described here. Now the Baudhāyana Sūtra, "When it is said that one goes on a journey for a limited period, it is, as it were, said that he does not go on a journey beyond a year. If he stays for more (than a year), he should while performing this Iṣṭi procure gold. (The procedure of) the Upavasatha day is well-known. When he has performed the morning Agnihotra-offering on the *parvan* day..."

If the Pavitreṣṭi is being performed for the first time, a Śrāddha-ceremony for the mothers should be performed after the Agnihotra-offering in the morning on the *parvan* day. Then (the rite of) choosing the priests (is performed). Then the Anvārambhaṇīyā Iṣṭi (is performed.) (Then the declaration of purpose). (**Fig. 26**). "I shall perform the Pavitreṣṭi to please the Supreme God." Then (the rites of) carrying forth of fires and adding fuel to the sacred fires (should be performed). **(Fig. 30).** (The sacrificer announces his intention,) "Now I shall perform a sacrifice today with a cake on eight potsherds to Agni Pavamāna, clarified butter, in a low tone, to Sarasvatī Priyā, a cake on eight potsherds to Agni Pāvaka, clarified butter, in a low tone [2B] to Savitṛ Satyaprasava, a cake on eight potsherds to Agni Śuci, clarified butter, in low tone, to Vāyu Niyutvat, a cake on eight potsherds to Agni Vratapati, clarified butter, in a low tone to Viṣṇu Śipiviṣṭa, a cake on twelve potsherds to Agni Vaiśvānara, clarified butter, in a low tone to Dadhikrāvan." *Saptadaśa vajra* (is to be used). (That is to say, the Hotṛ should modify the formula as *saptadaśena vajreṇa,* which he recites while sitting down after the invocation of the deities). The sacrifice is performed with paddy. (Regarding the rite of adding fuel to the fires), the option of *mamāgne* (is followed). The *anvāhārya caru* and a piece of gold are given away as *dakṣiṇā.* The sacrificer should adopt the vow at the last time. (That is to say after the oblations have been deposited within the altar, cf. KŚS. ii.8.2). At the time of choosing the Brahman-priest the sacrificer should say, "I am going to perform the Pavitreṣṭi." **(Fig. 31).** After the choosing of the Brahman-priest is done, (the Adhvaryu) consecrates the clarified butter as in the case of the Pūrṇāhuti. Then he takes some of it and cooks (makes hot) on the Gārhapatya fire. He cleanses the *agnihotrahavaṇī* and the spoon with the *darbha* blades, takes down the clarified butter, cleanses it by means of the two strainers, [3A] takes four spoonfuls in the ladle, goes near the Āhavanīya fire and offers it, while he is being touched by the sacrificer. **(Fig. 33).** He recites at that time, "*yena devāḥ.... svāhā.*" (Then the sacrificer says), "This is (offered) to the Pāvamānī deities. This is (now) not mine." Then the Adhvaryu again takes four spoonfuls and recites the verse, "*prājāpatyam pavitram ... svāhā.*" (Then the sacrificer says), "This is to Brahman. It is not mine." (Then the Adhvaryu) again takes four spoonfuls and offers (them) reciting, "*indraḥ sunītī* *saha mā ... svāhā.*" (The sacrificer then says), "This is to Indra and others, Sunītī and others. This is to Indra together with Sunītī, to Soma with Svasti, to Varuṇa [3B] with Samīcī, to king Yama with Pramṛṇas and to Jātavedas with Ūrjayantī. This is not mine." The Mantras beginning with *yena devāḥ* ... etc. are the three Mantras with which the offerings are to be made in each and every performance.

(The Adhvaryu) then (goes through) the carrying forth of the *praṇītā*-water, and other rites. (**Fig. 35**). At the time of placing the utensils, (he arranges for) forty-four potsherds, and five bowls for the cakes. Gold is the sacrificial fee. (**Fig. 34**). At the time of taking (the oblation material for) the *puroḍāśas*, he says, "I take this for Agni Pavamāna ... for Agni Pāvaka ... for Agni Śuci ... for Agni Vratapati and ... for Agni Vaiśvānara." (**Fig. 36**). At the time of sprinkling (the oblation material for purification he mentions in addition), "This belongs to Agni Pavamāna ... to Agni Pāvaka, ... to Agni Śuci... to Agni Vratapati, ... to Agni Vaiśvānara." At the time of besmearing the cakes with the clarified butter (cf. KŚS. ii. 8.14) he adds, "Go to Agni Pavamāna. Go to Agni Pāvaka. Go to Agni Śuci [4A]. Go to Agni Vratapati. Go to Agni Vaiśvānara." (**Fig. 78**).

(The Hotṛ goes to the Āhavanīya fire. He places his right foot near the northern buttock of the altar and the left foot near the right one. He should hold his folded hands upon his heart, and remain gazing on the conjunction of the sky and the earth. He should murmur the *namaḥkranda* formula) *namaḥ pravaktre...* etc. Then seventeen *sāmidhenī* verses (should be recited). (**Figs. 86 to 88**). The Hotṛ presses the ground with the span of his thumb and forefinger with (the formula modified as) "*saptadaśena vajreṇa...*"

(The *sāmidhenī* verses are :

1. *pra vo vājāḥ* ... ṚV. iii.27.1.

"In ladle dropping oil your food goes in oblation up to heaven, goes to the Gods in search of bliss."

2. *agna ā yāhi vītaye* ... ṚV. vi.16.10.

"Come, Agni, lauded, to the feast, come to the offering of the gifts. As priest be seated on the grass."

3. *taṃ tvā samidbhiḥ* ... ṚV. vi.16.11.

"With offerings meet let Agni bring the Fathers who support the Law. Let him announce oblations paid to Fathers and to Deities."

4. *sa naḥ pṛthu* ... ṚV. vi.16.12.

"For us thou winnest, Agni, God, heroic strength exceeding great. Far-spreading and of high renown."

5. *īḷenyo namasyaḥ* ... ṚV. iii.27.13.

"Meet to be lauded and adored, showing in beauty through the dark, Agni, the strong, is kindled well."

6. *vṛṣo agniḥ samidhyate* ... ṚV. iii.27.14.

"Agni is kindled as a bull, like a horse-bearer of the Gods. Men with oblations worship him."

7. *vṛṣaṇaṃ tvā vayam* ... ṚV. iii.27.15.

"Thee will we kindle as a bull, we who are Bulls overselves, Bull. Thee, Agni, shining mightily."

8. *agniṃ dūtaṃ vṛṇīmahe* ... ṚV i.12.1.

"We choose Agni the messenger, the herald, master of all wealth, well-skilled in this our sacrifice."

9. *samidhyamāno adhvare* ... ṚV. iii.27.4.

"Kindled at sacrifices he is Agni, hallower, meet for praise, with flame for hair : to him we seek."

After reciting this *Sāmidhenī* verse ending with) *śociṣkeśas tam īm aho3m*, (the Hotṛ should add the following two verses.)

10. *apām idaṃ nyayanam* ... TS. IV.vi.1.3.

"This is the place where waters meet; here is the gathering of the flood. Let thy shaft burn others than us : be thou cleanser, propitious unto us, " and

11. *namas te harase śociṣe* ... TS. IV.vi.1.3.

"Obeisance to thy wrath and glow : Obeisance to thy fiery flame : Let thy shot missiles burn others than us : be thou cleanser, propitious unto us."

(Then he recites the next *sāmidhenī* verses :)

12. *samiddho agna āhutaḥ* (... ṚV. v.28.5.

"Agni, invoked and kindled, serve the Gods, thou skilled in sacrifice : for thou art bearer of our gifts.

13. *ā juhotā* ... ṚV. v.28.6.

"Invoke and worship Agni while the sacrificial rite proceeds :

For offering-bearer choose ye him."

At the end of each *sāmidhenī* verse he adds "om.")

(When the deities are to be invoked,) the names Agni Pavamāna, Agni Pāvaka, Agni Śuci, Agni Vratapati and Agni Vaiśvānara should be uttered loudly. The others are *upāṃśu* deities, (i.e. their names should be uttered in a low tone.)

After having invoked the deities of the two *ājyabhāgas*, namely Agni and Soma, the Hotṛ says, "(O Agni), bring in Agni Pavamāna, bring in, in a low tone, Sarasvatī Priyā. [4B] Bring in Agni Pāvaka. Bring in, in a low tone, Savitṛ Satyaprasava. Bring in Agni Śuci. Bring in, in a low tone, Vāyu Niyutvat. Bring in Agni Vratapati. Bring in, in a low tone, Viṣṇu Śipiviṣṭa. Bring in Agni Vaiśvānara. Bring in, in a low tone Dadhikrāvan. (Bring in) gods, the drinkers of clarified butter etc." Then the five *prayājas*. As the last *prayāja* (the Hotṛ should recite) "*ye3 yajāmahe svāhā agniṃ svāhā somaṃ svāhā agniṃ pavamānaṃ svāhā*, in a low tone, *sarasvatīm priyāṃ svāhā agnim pāvakaṃ svāhā*, in a low tone, *savitāraṃ satyaprasavaṃ svāhā agniṃ śuciṃ svāhā*, in a low tone, *vāyuṃ niyutvataṃ svāhā agniṃ vratapatiṃ svāhā*, [5A] in a low tone, *viṣṇuṃ śipiviṣṭaṃ svāhā agniṃ vaiśvānaraṃ svāhā*, in a low tone, *dadhikrāvāṇaṃ svāhā devā* (*ājyapā* etc.) (**Figs. 96-100**). (The sacrificer follows with) "this is to Agni, to Soma, to Agni Pavamāna, to Sarasvatī Priyā, to Agni Pāvaka, to Savitṛ Satyaprasava, to Agni Śuci, to Vāyu Niyutvat, to Agni Vratapati, to Viṣṇu Śipiviṣṭa, to Agni Vaiśvānara, to Dadhikrāvan, Devas Ājyapas, (and the other deities of the *prayājas*)." The invitatory and oblatory verses of the two *ājyabhāga* offerings have the word *pāvaka* in them. The Adhvaryu gives out the call, "Do you recite the *puronuvākyā* for Agni." (The Hotṛ recites the verse) "*agnī rakṣāṃsi* ..." The Adhvaryu calls, "Do you recite the *yājyā* to Agni." The Hotṛ recites the verse "*ye yajāmahe agniṃ yat te...*" (After the offering to Agni, the sacrificer says,) "This is to Agni."

The Adhvaryu gives out the call, "Do you recite the *puronuvākyā* for Soma." The Hotṛ recites the verse, "*yo dhārayā...*" **[5B]** (At the Adhvaryu's call, he recites the *yājyā*) "*ye yajāmahe somam ā kalaśeṣu ...vau3 ṣaṭ,*" the sacrificer follows, "This is to Soma." (**Figs. 101-104**)

(Then begins the ritual of the principal offerings. The Adhvaryu gives out the call to the Hotṛ), "Do you recite the *puronuvākyā* for Agni Pavamāna." The Hotṛ recites the verse, "*agna āyūṃṣī pavase....*" (The Adhvaryu gives out the call), "Do you recite the *yājyā*." (The Hotṛ recites the verse), "*ye yajāmahe agniṃ pavamānam agne pavasva svāhā ... vau 3 ṣaṭ.*" The sacrificer follows, "This is to Agni Pavamāna (and not mine)."

The Adhvaryu then gives out the call, "Do you recite the *puronuvākyā* for, in a low tone, Sarasvatī Priyā." (The Hotṛ recites, in a low tone, the verse), "*uta naḥ priyā*" (loudly) "*om.*" The Adhvaryu gives out the call, "Do you recite the *yājyā,* in a low tone, to Sarasvatī Priyā." (The Hotṛ recites the verse), "*ye yajāmahe sarasvatīm* [6A] *priyām ... vau 3 ṣaṭ.*" The sacrificer follows, "This is to Sarasvatī Priyā and not mine."

The Adhvaryu gives out the call, "Do you recite the *puronuvākyā* for Agni Pāvaka." (The Hotṛ recites the verse), "*agne pāvaka rociṣam ...*" (The Adhvaryu then gives out the call), "Do you recite the *yājyā* to Agni Pāvaka." (The Hotṛ recites), "*ye yajāmahe agniṃ pāvakam ... vau 3 ṣaṭ.*" (The sacrificer follows), "This is to Agni Pāvaka and not mine."

(The Adhvaryu gives out a call), "Do you recite the

puronuvākyā, in a low tone, for Savitṛ Satyaprasava." (The Hotṛ recites), in a low tone, "*ā viśvadevaṃ satpatim* ..." (loudly) "*om.*" (The Adhvaryu gives out a call), "Do you recite the *yājyā,* in a low tone, "*savitāraṃ satyaprasavam*...." The Hotṛ recites, "*ye yajāmahe,*" in a low tone, "*savitāraṃ satyaprasavam*..."(loudly) "*vau 3 ṣaṭ*" (The sacrificer follows), "This is to Savitṛ Satyaprasava and not mine."

(The Adhvaryu gives out a call to the Hotṛ), " Do you recite the *puronuvākyā* for Agni Śuci. (The Hotṛ recites), "*agniḥ śuciḥ vratatamaḥ*..." (The Adhvaryu gives out a call to the Hotṛ), "Do you recite the *yājyā* to Agni Śuci." (The Hotṛ recites), "*ye yajāmahe agniṃ śuciṁ*..." (The sacrificer follows with), "This is to Agni Śuci and not mine."(The Adhvaryu gives out a call) "Do you recite the *puronuvākyā,* in a low tone, for Vāyu Niyutvaṭ." (The Hotṛ recites in a low tone the verse), "*vāyur agregā yajñaprīḥ* ..." (loudly) "*om.*" (The Adhvaryu gives out a call), "Do you recite the *yājyā* (in a low tone) to Vāyu Niyutvat." **[7A]** (The Hotṛ recites) "*ye yajāmahe,*" in a low tone, "*vāyuṃ niyutvantaṃ vāyo śukraḥ* ..." (loudly) "*vau 3 ṣaṭ.*" The sacrificer follows, "This is to Vāyu Niyutvat and not mine."

The Adhvaryu gives out a call to the Hotṛ, "Do you recite the *puronuvākyā* for Agni Vratapati." (The hotṛ recites the verse), "*tvam agne vratapā asi ... om.*" (The Adhvaryu gives out a call), "Do you recite the *yājyā* for Agni Vratapati." (The Hotṛ recites the verse), "*ye yajāmahe agniṃ vratapatiṃ yad vo vayam ... vau 3 ṣaṭ.*" The sacrificer follows, "This is to Agni Vratapati and not mine."

(The Adhvaryu gives out a call to the Hotṛ), "Do you recite the *puronuvākyā,* in a low tone, for Viṣṇu Śipiviṣṭa." (The Hotṛ recites in a low tone) "*pra tat te adya*...." **[7B]** (loudly) "*om.*" (The Adhvaryu gives out a call) "Do you recite the *yājyā,*" in a low tone, "to Viṣṇu Śipiviṣṭa." The Hotṛ recites "*ye yajāmahe,*" in a low tone, "*viṣṇuṃ śipiviṣṭaṃ kim it te viṣṇo* ..." (loudly) "...

vau 3 ṣaṭ.'' The sacrificer follows, ''This is to Viṣṇu Śipiviṣṭa and not mine.''

(The Adhvaryu gives out a call to the Hotṛ), ''Do you recite the *puronuvākyā* for Agni Vaiśvānara.'' (The Hotṛ recites the verse), *vaiśvānaro nu ūtyā... om.*'' (The Adhvaryu gives out a call), ''Do you recite the yājyā to Agni Vaiśvānara.'' (The Hotṛ recites), ''*ye yajāmahe agniṃ vaiśvānaraṃ pṛṣṭo divi... vau 3 ṣaṭ.*'' (the sacrificer follows), ''This is to Agni Vaiśvānara and not mine.''

(The Adhvaryu gives out a call to the Hotṛ), ''Do you recite the *puronuvākyā,* in a low tone, for Dadhikrāvan.'' **[8A]** (The Hotṛ recites in a low tone) ''*dadhikrāvṇo akāriṣam* ...'' (loudly) ''*om.*'' (The Adhvaryu gives out a call), ''Do you recite the *yājyā,* in a low tone, to Dadhikrāvan.'' (The Hotṛ recites) ''*ye yajāmahe,* in a low tone, *''dadhikrāvāṇam ā dadhikrāḥ''* ... (loudly) ''*vau 3 ṣaṭ.*'' (The sacrificer follows), ''This is to Dadhikrāvan and not mine.'' **(Figs. 105-109)**

(The Adhvaryu gives out a call to the Hotṛ), ''Do you recite the *puronuvākyā,* in a low tone, for Agni *sviṣṭakṛt.*'' (The Hotṛ recites), ''*juṣṭo damūnā atithir duroṇe ...om.*''

The adhvaryu takes out clarified butter from the vessel by means of the spoon. For *sviṣṭakṛt,* the cuttings are taken from the northern part of the cakes only and not from the clarified butter (in the *dhruvā* ladle). **[8B]** He takes a cutting from each of the cakes offered to Agni Pavamāna etc. in another pot and then puts it into the *juhū* ladle. For the *pañcāvattins* (those who offer in five cuttings), he takes two cuttings of each cake and covers it twice with clarified butter in a common diminution. He does not touch with clarified butter that part of the oblation from which the cuttings are taken **(Fig. 112)** and he does not go beyond. He sits at his own place. He takes clarified butter from the vessel and offers subsidiary oblations with the spoon. He offers with ''*pavamānaḥ suvarjanaḥ...*'' The sacrificer follows, ''This is to Pavamāna Suvarjana, Pavitra Vicarṣaṇa, Potṛ and not mine.'' With ''*punantu mā devajanāḥ...*''

the Adhvaryu offers an oblation. The sacrificer follows, "This is to Devajanas, Manu and Viśvāyu and not mine." With *"jātavedaḥ pavitravat..."* [9A] he offers an oblation. The sacrificer follows, "This is to Jātavavedas Agni and not mine."

With *"yat te pavitram..."* the Adhvaryu offers to Agni. The sacrificer follows, "This is to Agni and not mine." With *"ubhābhyāṃ deva savitaḥ"* the Adhvaryu offers an oblation. The sacrificer follows, "This is to Deva Savitṛ, Brahman and not mine." Then the Adhvaryu offers an oblation with *"vaiśvadevī punatī devī..."* The sacrificer follows, "This is to Vaiśvadevī Punatī and not mine." The Adhvaryu offers with *"vaiśvānaro raśmibhiḥ ..."* The sacrificer follows, "This is to Vaiśvānara Vāteṣira Dyāvāpṛthivī Ṛtāvarī and not mine." [9B] The Adhvaryu offers an oblation with *"bṛhadbhiḥ savitas tṛbhiḥ..."* The sacrificer follows, "This is to Savitṛ Agni and not mine." The Adhvaryu offers an oblation with *"yena devā apunata..."* The sacrificer follows, "This is to Brahman and not mine." The Adhvaryu offers an oblation with *"yaḥ pāvamānīr adhyeti..."* The sacrificer follows, "This is to Pāvamānī and not mine." The Adhvaryu offers an oblation with *"pāvamānīr yo adhyeti...."* The sacrificer follows, "this is to Pāvamānī and not mine." The Adhvaryu offers an oblation with *"pāvamānīḥ svastyayanīḥ..."* [10A] The sacrificer follows, "This is to Pāvamānī and not mine." The Adhvaryu offers an oblation with *"pāvamānīr diśantu naḥ..."* The sacrificer follows, "this is to Pāvamānī and not mine." The Adhvaryu offers an oblation with *"pāvamānīḥ svastyayanīḥ...,"* The sacrificer follows, "This is to Pāvamānī and mine." The Adhvaryu offers an oblation with *"yena devāḥ..."* The sacrificer follows, "This is to Pāvamānī and not mine." The Adhvaryu offers an oblation with *"prājāpatyaṃ pavitram...* The sacrificer follows, "This is to Brahman and not mine." The Adhvaryu offers an oblation with *"indraḥ sunītī saha mā ..."* [10B] The sacrificer follows, "This is to Indra and others, Sunītī and others and not mine." Or he says, "This is to Indra together with Sunītī, Soma together with Svasti, Varuṇa together with Samīcī, Yama together with Pramṛṇas, Jātavedas together with Ūrjayantī and not mine''.

Then the Adhvaryu crosses the altar and causes the Āgnīdhra to announce (and then gives out a call to the Hotṛ), ''recite the *yājyā* to Agni Sviṣṭakṛt.'' (The Hotṛ then recites the usual formula) ''*ye yajāmahe agniṃ sviṣṭakṛtam* ...'' joining to that the names of all the divinities which are invoked, in genitive case. The names of the *upāṃśu* deities, viz. Sarasvatī Priyā, Savitṛ Satyaprasava, **[11A]** Vāyu Niyutvat etc. he utters in a low tone. He joins to it the verse *mārjālyo mṛjyate ... vau 3 ṣaṭ.* (The Adhvaryu offers the oblation to Agni Sviṣṭakṛt) (**Fig. 113**). The sacrificer follows, ''This is to Agni Sviṣṭakṛt and not mine.'' For the *prāśitra* (i.e. the portion intended for the Brahman), he takes the portion only from the first cake. (**Fig. 114**). The procedure of the *iḍā* is well-konwn. (**Figs. 115-120**). The sacrificer then places the *anvāhārya caru* (within the altar) and gives a hundred *mānas* of gold. He follows it with ''*prajāpater bhāgo'si* ...'' He says, **[11B]** ''I give an equal share of this rice and this gold to you, i.e,. the Brahman and the other priests for the accomplishment of this Pavitreṣṭi.'' **(Figs. 121, 122)**

The priests Brahman, Hotṛ, Adhvaryu and Āgnīdhra accept it saying, ''*dyaus tvā dadātu pṛthivī tvā pratigṛhṇātu*'' and ''*ko'dāt*'' etc.

At the time of separating the ladles, the *juhū* is taken to the east, by means of the right hand with the palm turned upwards and the *upabhṛt* to the west, by means of the left hand with the palm turned downwards, with the formulas ''*agneḥ pavamānasya ... ujjitim* ... and *agniḥ pavamānaḥ .... apanudantu ...* '' respectively (KŚS. iii.5.17-21).

In the *sūktavāka* **[12A]** after the *ājyabhāga* offerings, the Hotṛ should add at the relevant point the names of all the principal divinities in the nominative case and utter the words *idaṃ havir ajuṣatāvīvṛdhata maho jyāyo'kṛta* after each name. In the case of the *upāṃśu* divinites, only the words *idaṃ haviḥ* and *maho jyāyaḥ* he utters in a loud tone and all the other words he utters in a low tone. Then he should recite *devā ājyapā* ... etc. Then the rites upto *patnīsaṃyāja* are performed as usual. (**Figs. 131-135**). Then the screen (used for the *patnīsaṃyāja* offering) is removed. Before the offering to Agni Gārhapatya, **[12 B]** the Adhvaryu should offer the subsidiary oblations of spoonfuls of clarified butter.

(The mantras accompanying these oblations are found at TBr. III.vii.12.1 to 6). (The Adhvaryu offers the first oblation with the mantra) "O resplendent gods, whatever act, causing anger to the gods we might have committed, may the sons of Aditi absolve me from that sin with the truthfulness of the truth : *svāhā.*" (The sacrificer then says), "This is to the gods Ādityas and not mine."(1)

(The Adhvaryu offers the second oblation with the mantra) "O gods, whatever lie we might have uttered being desirous of life may the Gārhapatya fire absolve me from that sin. Whatever evil acts we might have committed, may he render me sinless : *svāhā.*" (Then the sacrificer says), "This is to Agni Gārhapatya and not mine."(2)

(The Adhvaryu offers the third oblation with the mantra) "With the truthfulness, O Dyāvāpṛthivī, with the truthfulness, O Sarasvatī, may you absolve me from the sin which I have incurred and which is inflicted upon us by the others : *svāhā.*" (The sacrificer then says), "This is to Dyāvāpṛthivī and Sarasvatī. This is not mine."(3)

(The Adhvaryu offers the fourth oblation with the mantra) "From the sin which has been caused to us by the imprecation of our relatives or brothers, or of the elder ones or of the younger ones and also from the sin in respect of god which we might have committed unknowingly; **[13A]** may you, O Agni Jātavedas, absolve us : *svāhā.*" (The sacrificer then says), "This is to Agni Jātavedas and not mine."(4)

(The Adhvaryu offers the fifth oblation with the mantra)

"Whatever sin we might have committed through our speech or mind or through the hands or thighs or legs or through the penis; may Agni Gārhapatya absolve me from that sin. Whatever evil acts we might have committed; may he render me sinless : *svāhā*. The sacrificer then says), "This is to Agni Gārhapatya and not mine."(5)

(The Adhvaryu offers the sixth oblation with the mantra) "Whatever evil acts I might have committed with my hands indulging in the prohibited acts regarding the (sensual) organs; may the two Apsarasas as viz. Dūrepaśyā and Rāṣṭrabhṛt pay back the debts (thereof): *svāhā*." (The sacrificer then says), "This is to the two Apsarasas viz. Dūrepaśyā and Rāṣṭrabhṛt. This is not mine."(6)

(The Adhvaryu offers the seventh oblation with the mantra) "Whatever debt I might have incurred by not gambling properly or whatever I have swallowed not willing to give away to people; may Agni Gārhapatya absolve me from that sin. Whatever evil acts we might have committed; may he render me sinless : *svāhā*" **[13 B]**. (The sacrificer then says), "This is to Agni Gārhapatya and not mine."(7)

(The Adhvaryu offers the eighth oblation with the mantra) "Whatever sin my mother or my father might have committed when I was in the embryonic stage; may Agni Gārhapatya absolve me from that sin. Whatever evil acts we might have committed; may he render me sinless : *svāhā*." (The sacrificer then says), "This is to Agni Gārhapatya and not mine."(8)

(The Adhvaryu offers the ninth oblation with the mantra) "Even though I might have caused trouble to my father and mother while being a son sucking happily, I have not harmed my parents by that. Therefore, O Agni, I become free of that debt : *svāhā*." (The sacrificer then says), "This to Agni and not mine."(9)

(The Adhvaryu offers the tenth oblation with the mantra) "Whatever harm we might have caused to the mid-region, to the earth or to the heaven, whatever to the mother or to the father; may Agni Gārhapatya absolve me from that sin. Whatever evil acts we might have committed; may he render me sinless : *svāhā.*" (The sacrificer then says), "This is to Agni Gārhapatya and not mine."(10)

(The Adhvaryu offers the eleventh oblation with the mantra) "Whatever sin--new or old--we might have committed causing injury intentionally or un-intentionally or by imprecations [14A] may Agni Gārhapatya absolve me from that sin. Whatever evil acts we might have committed; may he render me sinless : *svāhā.*" (The sacrificer then says), "This is to Agni Gārhapatya and not mine."(11)

(The Adhvaryu offers the twelfth oblation with the mantra) "I overcome the evil leading to sin. I abandon the impurities in the highest abode. I indeed ascend to the world of well-doers, where the well-doers alone can reach and not the evil-doers : *svāhā.*" (The sacrificer then says), "This is to Agni Gārhapatya and not mine."(12)

(The Adhvaryu offers the thirteenth oblation with the mantra) "The gods wiped off this sin unto Trita. Trita wiped it off unto men. Whatever little of it may have reached me; may Agni Gārhapatya absolve me from that sin. Whatever evil acts we might have committed; may he render me sinless : *svāhā* ." (The sacrificer then says), "This is to Agni Gārhapatya and not mine."(13)

(The Adhvaryu offers the fourteenth oblation with the mantra) "The waters produced in the heaven, those produced in the waters and from the plants and also the waters produced from the fire--may all these purifying ones purify us : *svāhā.*" [14B] (The sacrificer then says), "This is to the purifying waters and not mine."(14)

(The Adhvaryu offers the fifteenth oblation with the mantra) "O Waters, whatever evil--new or old--we might commit at night or in the day; may you, the golden colour ones, purify us off it : *svāhā.*" (Then the sacrificer says), "This is to the golden colour waters and not mine."(15)

(The Adhvaryu offers the sixteenth oblation with the mantra) "O Varuṇa, hear this call of mine. Be gracious unto me this day.

Longing for help I yearn for thee : *svāhā.*" (The sacrificer then says), "This is to Varuṇa and not mine."(16)

(The Adhvaryu offers the seventeenth oblation with the mantra) "I come to you paying homage with this prayer. The sacrificer wishes for this with his oblations. Varuṇa, stay you here and be not angry. Do not steal our life from us, O wide-ruler, *svāhā.*" (The sacrificer then says), "This is to Varuṇa and not mine."(17)

(The Adhvaryu offers the eighteenth oblation with the mantra) "O Agni, wise one, put far away from us the anger of God Varuṇa. O Best Sacrificer, the brightest and refulgent one, remove far from us all those who hate us : *svāhā.*" (The sacrificer then says), "This is to Agni and Varuṇa and not mine."(18)

[15A] (The Adhvaryu offers the nineteenth oblation with the mantra) "O Agni, be you nearest to us, our closest friend now at the day-break. Reconcile Varuṇa to us, be bounteous. Show us compassion and be swift to hear us : *svāhā.*" (The sacrificer then says), "This is to Agni and Varuṇa and not mine."(19)

(The Adhvaryu offers the twentieth oblation with the mantra) "O Agni, you are this. It is what we have in mind that you are this. Being this, you carry our oblations and being this only, do place the beneficial unto us : *svāhā.*" (The sacrificer then says), "This is to Agni and not mine."(20)

Then the rites beginning with the offering to Agni Gṛhapati and ending with the gratification of the Brāhamaṇas should be gone through. The rest of the ritual other than that presented here is like that of the full moon sacrifice. Thus the Pavitreṣṭi comes to an end.

APPENDIX II

Sanskrit Text of the *Pavitreṣṭiprayoga*

Description of MS

Title -	Pavitreṣṭi (vāja.), BORI No. 422 of 1883-84		
Extent -	Foll. 15	**Script -**	Devanāgarī
Date -	Not mentioned	**Author -**	Not mentioned
Scribe -	Not mentioned		

Method Adopted for Transliteration

1. Vertical strokes as punctuation marks given in the MS have generally been retained. Sometimes they have been deleted or added, wherever found necessary. However, no reference to the deletion or the addition has been made in the notes appended to the transliterated text.

2. A portion copied wrongly has been deleted in the MS by putting small vertical strokes on the top of each letter. The transliterated text has only the corrected portion.

3. *Anusvāra* (*ṃ*) occurring before the punctuation mark is replaced by *m*.

4. MS does not use *avagraha*. It is denoted by an apostrophy, wherever necessary.

5. The verb form *gacha*, a usual reading for *gaccha* occurring in the MSs of Śrautasūtras, has been retained.

6. Words at the end of the mantras are modified in the MS, according to the way they are recited. The reading in the MS is generally retained.

7. The portions omitted or abbreviated in the MS are supplied in brackets.

8. The notes appended to the transliterated text show the readings in the MS.

[1A] atha pavitreṣṭiprārambhaḥ / [1B] śrī gaṇeśāya namaḥ / atha pavitreṣṭiḥ sā ca parvaṇi[1] kāryā / sā sarvapāpakṣayāya /

vaiśvānarīṃ vrātapatīṃ pavitreṣṭim ṛtāv ṛtau /
mṛgāreṣṭiṃ ca kurvāṇaḥ punāty ā viṃśatiṃ kulam //

iti yajñagāthā / daśa· pūrvān daśāparān ātmānaṃ caikaviṃśatiṃ[2] *paṅktiṃ ca punāti* (BaudhŚS. 28.2) iti bhagavatā baudhāyanenoktam / *ṛtāv ṛtāv* iti vīpsādarśanān nityatvam eṣām / tathā ca

pavitreṣṭyā viśudhyanti[3] *sarve ghorāḥ pratigrahāḥ /*

yadā pratigrahajanitapāpakṣayārthaṃ pavitreṣṭiḥ kriyate tadā kāmyatvād anvārambhaṇīyā kartavyā / yadā nityatvāt prativarṣaṃ kriyate tadā prathamaprayoge evā[4]nvārambhaṇīyā / tatra mitravindāpavitre[5]ṣṭyoḥ sahaivoktatvāt / svaśākhāyāṃ pavitreṣṭe[6] [2A] r abhāvād baudhāyanādyuktapavitreṣṭir apy abhidhīyate / atha bodhāyanasūtram / *atho etat so'parimitaṃ pravasati na saṃvatsaram atipravasatīty* evedam uktaṃ bhavati *sa u ced atipravaset pavitreṣṭyā yajetety etayeṣṭyā yakṣyamāṇa*[7] *upakalpayate hiraṇyaṃ tasyāḥ prajñāta upavasatho'tha prātar hute'gnihotre* (BaudhŚS. 28.2) / parvaṇi prātar agnihotrahomānantaraṃ pavitreṣṭau prathamaprayoge mātṛśrāddham / ṛtvigvaraṇam / tato'nvārambhaṇīyā / *oṃ tat sat parameśvaraprītyarthaṃ pavitreṣṭyāhaṃ yakṣye* / punaruddharaṇam (KŚS. iv.13.1) / agnyanvādhānam / *agniṃ pavamānam aṣṭākapālena puroḍāśena* / upāṃśu / *sarasvatīṃ priyām*[8] / uccaiḥ *ājyena / agniṃ pāvakam aṣṭāka* [2B] *pā(lena puroḍāśe)na* / upāṃ(śu) *savitāraṃ satyaprasavam* / uccaiḥ *ājyena / agniṃ śucim aṣṭākapā(lena puroḍāśe)na* / upāṃ(śu) / *vāyuṃ niyutvantam*[9] / uccaiḥ *ājyena / agniṃ vratapatim aṣṭāka(pālena puroḍāśe)na* / upāṃ(śu) *viṣṇuṃ śipiviṣṭam* / uccaiḥ *ājyena / agniṃ vaiśvānaraṃ dvādaśakapāle (na) pu(roḍāśe)na* upāṃ(śu) *dadhikrāvāṇam / ājyenety* uccaiḥ / *sadyo'haṃ yakṣye*[10] / saptadaśo vajraḥ / vrīhibhir yāgaḥ / mamāgneḥ pakṣaḥ (KŚS. ii.1.3) / anvāhāryahiraṇyaṃ dakṣiṇā / uttame kāle vratopāyanam / brahmavaraṇe *pavitreṣṭyāhaṃ yakṣye*[10] / brahmavaraṇānantaram / pūrṇāhutivad ājyaṃ saṃskṛtya / nirupyājyaṃ gārhapatye'dhiśritya / havanīyaṃ sruvaṃ ca samṛjya darbhair udvāsyotpūya pavitrābhyām / havaṇyāṃ caturgṛ [3A] hītaṃ gṛhītvā āhavanīyasamīpaṃ gatvā yajamānānvārabdhe juhoti /

yena devāḥ pavitreṇātmānaṃ punate sadā /
tena sahasradhāreṇa pāvamānyaḥ punantu mā (TBr. I.iv.8.6)

svāhā // idaṃ pāvamānībhyo na ma(ma) / aparaṃ caturgṛ(hītaṃ gṛhī)tvā /

prājāpatyaṃ pavitraṃ śatodyāmaṃ hiraṇmayam /
tena brahmavido vayaṃ pūtaṃ brahma punīmahe (TBr. I.iv.8.6) *svāhā // idaṃ brahmaṇe na ma(ma) /* aparaṃ caturgṛhītvā juhoti /

indraḥ sunītī saha mā punātu soma(ḥ) svastyā varuṇaḥ samīcyā /
yamo rājā pramṛṇābhiḥ punātu mā jātavedā morjayantyā punātu (TBr. I.iv.8.6) *svāhā //*

idam indrādibhyaḥ sunītyādibhyo na mama / idam indrāya sunītyā sahitāya somāya svastyā sahitāya varuṇāya sa [3B] *mīcyā sahitāya yamā(ya) rājñe pramṛṇābhiḥ sahitāya jātavedasa ūrjayantyā sahitāya na mama /* ete *yena devāḥ* iti trayo homamantrāḥ / pratiprayogamātre / tataḥ praṇītāpraṇayanādi pātrāsādane kapālāni 44 / puroḍāśapātryaḥ pañca / hiraṇyaṃ dakṣiṇā / grahaṇe / *agnaye pavamānāya juṣṭaṃ gṛ(hṇā)mi / agnaye pāvakāya ju(ṣṭaṃ gṛhṇā)mi / agnaye śucaye ju(ṣṭaṃ gṛhṇā)mi / agnaye vratapataye ju(ṣṭaṃ gṛhṇā)mi / agnaye vaiśvānarāya ju(ṣṭaṃ gṛhṇā)mi /* prokṣaṇe tv adhikaḥ nirdeśaḥ[11] / *idam agneḥ pavamānasya / idam agneḥ pāvakasya / idam agneḥ śuceḥ / idam agner vratapateḥ / idam agner vaiśvānarasya /* prāṇadāne / *agniṃ pavamānaṃ gacha/ agniṃ pāvakaṃ gacha / agniṃ śuciṃ* [4A] *gacha / agniṃ vratapatiṃ gacha / agniṃ vaiśvānaraṃ gacha / namaḥ pravaktra* (Hautrika 1.1.1) ityādi saptadaśa sāmidhenyaḥ / saptadaśena vajreṇe'ty avabādhanam (cf. KŚS. iii.1.7) /

śociṣkeśas tam īm aho3m (ṚV. iii.27.4) /
apām idaṃ nyayanaṃ samudrasya niveśanam /
anyaṃ te asmat tapantu hetayaḥ

pāvako asmabhyaṃ śivo bhavo3m (TS. IV.vi.1.3) //
namas te harase śociṣe namas te astv arciṣe /
anyaṃ te asmat tapantu hetayaḥ
pāvako asmabhyaṃ śivo bhavo3m (TS. IV.vi.1.3) // *samiddho agna āhuta* (TS. II.v.8.6) ityādi[12] / *agniḥ pavamāno'gniḥ pāvako'gniḥ śucir agnir vratapatir agnir vaiśvānara* ity uccaiḥ / anyā upāṃśu devatāḥ / ājyabhāgāv āvāhya / *a(gnim agna ā3 vaha) so(mam ā3 vaha) agniṃ pavamānam ā3 vaha* / upāṃ(śu) / *sarasvatīṃ priyām* / *ā vahe* [4B] ty uccaiḥ / *agniṃ pāvakam ā3 vaha* / upāṃ(śu) *savitāraṃ satyaprasavam* uccaiḥ *ā3 vaha* / *agniṃ śucim ā3 vaha* / upāṃ(śu) *vāyuṃ niyutvantam* / uccaiḥ *ā3 vaha* / *agniṃ vratapatim ā3 vaha* / upāṃ(śu) / *viṣṇuṃ śipiviṣṭam* / uccaiḥ *ā3 vaha* / *agniṃ vaiśvānaram ā3 vaha* / upāṃ(śu) *dadhikrāvāṇam* / uccaiḥ *ā3 vaha* / *devān ājyapān (ā3 vaha / agniṃ hotrāyāvaha / svaṃ mahimānam ā vaha / ā ca vaha jātavedaḥ suyajā ca yaja)* (Hautrika 1.3) ityādi pañca prayājāḥ / uttame prayāje / *ye3 yajāmahe svāhāgniṃ svāhā somaṃ svāhāgniṃ pavamānaṃ svāhā* / upāṃ(śu) *sarasvatīṃ priyām* uccaiḥ / *svāhāgniṃ pāvakaṃ svāhā* / upāṃ(śu) *savitāraṃ satyaprasavam* / uccai(ḥ) *svāhāgniṃ śuciṃ svāhā* / upāṃ(śu) *vāyuṃ niyutvantam* / uccai(ḥ) *svāhāgniṃ vratapatiṃ svāhā* [5A] upāṃ(śu) *viṣṇuṃ śipiviṣṭam* / uccaiḥ *svāhāgniṃ vaiśvānaraṃ svāhā* / upāṃ(śu) *dadhikrāvāṇam* / uccaiḥ *svāhā devā (ājyapā juṣāṇā agna ājyasya vyantu)* (Hautrika 1.4.16) ityādi / *idam agnaye somāyāgnaye pavamānāya sarasvatyai priyā(yā) (a)gnaye pāvakāya savitre satyaprasavāyāgnaye śucaye vāyave niyutvate'gnaye vratapataye viṣṇave śipiviṣṭāyāgnaye vaiśvānarāya dadhikrāvṇe devebhya ājyape (bhyo'gnaye sviṣṭakṛte ca na mameti* tyāgaṃ vidhāya) *pañca (mama na tasya kiñcana yo'smān dveṣṭi yaṃ ca vayaṃ dviṣmaḥ annādo bhūyāsam* iti / KID. p.57*)* / pāvakavantāv ājyabhāgau / *agnaye'nubrū(hi) agnī rakṣāṃsi sedhati*[13] *śukraśocir amartyaḥ* / *śuciḥ pāvaka īḍyo3ṃ* / (TBr. II.iv.1.6) *agniṃ yaja* / *ye3yajāmahe'gniṃ yat te pavitram arciṣy agne vitatam antarā* / *brahma tena punīmahā3* (TBr. I.iv.8.2)*vau3ṣaṭ* / *idam agnaye (na mama) somāyā'(nubrūhi)*

/ *yo ḍhārayā pāvakayā pari prasyan* [5B] *date sutaḥ / indur aśvo na kṛtvi o3m* (ṚV. IX.101.2) / *ye 3 ya(jāma)he somam ā kalaśeṣu dhāvati pavitre pari ṣicyate / ukthair yajñeṣu vardhatā3i* (ṚV. IX.17.4) *vau3(ṣaṭ) / idaṃ somā (ya na mama)* / atha pradhānasya / *agnaye pavamānāyānu(brūhi) agna āyūṃṣi pavasa ā suvo'rjam iṣaṃ ca naḥ / ā re bādhasva ducchuno3m* (TS. I.iii.14.7) / *agniṃ pavamānaṃ yaja / ye3 yajā(ma)he'gniṃ pavamānam agne pavasva svapā asme varcaḥ suvīryaṁ / dadhat poṣaṃ rayiṃ mayī3* (TS. I.iii.14.8) *vau(3ṣaṭ) / idam agnaye pavamānā(ya na mama)* / upāṃ(śu) *sarasvatyai priyāyai* / uccai(r) *anubrūhi* / upāṃ(śu) *uta naḥ priyā*[14] *priyāsu saptasvasā sujuṣṭā / sarasvatī stomyābhūt* (TB. II.iv.6.1) / uccaiḥ *om* upāṃ(śu) *sarasvatīṃ priyām / yajety* uccaiḥ / *ye3 ya(jāma)he sarasvatīṃ* [6A] *priyām imā juvhānā yuṣmad ā namobhiḥ prati stomaṃ sarasvati*[15] *juṣasva / tava śarman priyatame dadhānā upa stheyāma śaraṇaṃ na vṛkṣam3* (TB. II.iv.6.1) / *vau3(ṣaṭ) idaṃ sarasvatyai priyāyai na (mama) agnaye pāvakāyānubrūhi / agne pāvaka rociṣā mandrayā deva jihvayā / ā devān vakṣi yakṣi co3m* (TS. I.iii.14.8) *agniṃ pāvakaṃ yaja / ye3 ya(jāma)he'gniṃ pāvakaṃ sa naḥ pāvaka dīdivo'gne devān ihāvaha / upa yajñaṃ haviś ca nā3* (TS. I.iii.14.8) *vau3(ṣaṭ) idam agnaye pāvakāya (na mama)* / upāṃ(śu) / *savitre satyaprasavāya / anubrū(hīty* u)ccaiḥ / upāṃ(śu) / *ā viśvadevaṃ satpatiṃ sūktair adyāvṛṇīmahe / satyasavaṃ savitāram* (TS. III.iv.11.2) / uccaiḥ / *om* / upāṃ(śu) *savitāraṃ satyaprasavam / yajety* uccaiḥ / *ye3 ya(jāma)he* [6B] upāṃ(śu) / *savitāraṃ satyaprasavam ā satyena rajasā vartamāno niveśayan na mṛtaṃ martyaṃ ca / hiraṇyayena savitā rathenādevo yāti bhuvanā vipaśyā3 n* (TS. III.iv.11.2) / uccaiḥ *vau3(ṣaṭ) idaṃ savitre satyaprasavāya (na mama) agnaye śucaye'nubrūhi / agniḥ śucir vratatamaḥ śucir vipraḥ śuciḥ kaviḥ / śucī rocata āhuto3m* (TS. I.iii.14.8) / *agniṃ śuciṃ yaja / ye3 ya(jāma)he'gniṃ śucim ud agne śucayas tava śukrā bhrājanta īrate/ tava jyotīṃṣy arcayā3* (TS. I.iii.14.8) *vau3(ṣaṭ) idam agnaye śucaye (na mama)* upāṃ(śu) *vāyave niyutvate / anubrūhīty* uccaiḥ / upāṃ(śu) *vāyur agregā yajñaprīḥ sākaṃgan manasā yajñam / śivo niyudbhiḥ śivābhiḥ* (TBr. II.iv.7.6)/ uccaiḥ / *om* upāṃ(śu) *vāyuṃ niyutvantam* / [7A] *yajety* uccaiḥ / *ye3 ya(jāma)he* upāṃ(śu) *vāyuṃ niyutvantaṃ vāyo śukro ayāmi te madhvo agraṃ diviṣṭiṣu / ā yāhi somapītaye svāruho deva niyutvatā* (TBr. II.iv.7.6-7) / uccaiḥ *vau3(ṣaṭ) idaṃ vāyave niyutvate na (mama) / agnaye vratapataye'nubrūhi / tvam agne vratapā asi deva ā martyeṣv ā / tvaṃ yajñeṣv īḍyo3 m* (TS. I.i.14.4) / *agniṃ vratapatiṃ yaja / ye3 ya(jāma)he'gniṃ vratapatiṃ yad vo vayaṃ pra mināma vratāni viduṣāṃ devā aviduṣṭarāsaḥ / agniṣ ṭad viśvam ā pṛṇāti vidvān yebhir devān*[16] *ṛtubhiḥ kalpayātī3* (TS. I.i.14.4) *vau3(ṣaṭ) / idam agnaye vratapataye na mama* / upāṃ(śu) *viṣṇave śipiviṣṭāya / anubrūhīty* uccaiḥ / upāṃśu *pra tat te adya śipiviṣṭa nāmāryaḥ śaṃsāmi vayunāni vidvān / taṃ tvā gṛṇāmi* [7B] *tavasaṃ tavīyān*[17] *kṣayantam asya rajasaḥ parāke* (TS. II.ii.12.5) / uccaiḥ upāṃ(śu) *viṣṇuṃ śipiviṣṭam / yajety* uccaiḥ / *ye3 ya(jāmahe)* upāṃ(śu) *śipiviṣṭaṃ kim it te viṣṇo paricakṣyaṃ bhūt pra yad vavakṣe śipiviṣṭo asmi / mā varpo asmad apa gūha etad yad anyarūpaḥ samithe babhūthā3* (TS. II.ii.12.5) *vau3(ṣaṭ) idaṃ viṣṇave śipiviṣṭāya (na mama) agnaye vaiśvānarāyānubrūhi vaiśvānaro na utyā pra yātu*[18] *parāvataḥ / agnir ukthena vāhaso3m* (TS. I.v.11.1) / *agniṃ vaiśvānaraṃ yaja / ye 3 ya(jāma)he'gniṃ vaiśvānaraṃ pṛṣṭo divipṛṣṭo agniḥ pṛthivyāṃ pṛṣṭo viśvā oṣadhīr ā viveśa / vaiśvānaraḥ sahasā pṛṣṭo agniḥ sa no divā sa riṣaḥ pātu naktāṃ3* (TS. I.v.11.1) *vau(3ṣaṭ) idam agnaye vaiśvānarāya (na mama)* upāṃ(śu) *dadhikrāvṇe / anu* [8A] *brū(hīty*u) ccaiḥ upāṃ(śu) *dadhikrāvṇo akāriṣaṃ jiṣṇor aśvasya vājinaḥ / surabhi no mukhā karat pra ṇa āyūṃṣi tāriṣat* (TS. I.v.11.4) / uccaiḥ *om* upāṃ(śu) *dadhikrāvāṇam / yajety* uccaiḥ / *ye3 ya(jāma)he* / upāṃ(śu) / *dadhikrāvāṇam ā dadhikrāḥ śavasā pañca kṛṣṭīḥ sūrya iva jyotiṣāpastatānā / sahasrasāḥ śatasā vājy arvā pṛṇaktu madhvā sam imā vacāṃsīṃ* (TS. I.v.11.4) *vau(3ṣaṭ) / idaṃ dadhikrāvṇe na mama / agnaye sviṣṭakṛte'nubrūhi / juṣṭo damūnā atithir duroṇa imaṃ no yajñam upa yāhi vidvān / viśvā agne'bhiyujo vihatyā śatrūyatām ā bharā bhojanāno3m* (TBr. II.iv.1.1) / sruveṇa sthālīto'pastāraḥ / yāvad dhaviruttarārdhāt sviṣṭakṛta eva homo nājyād aśeṣā [8B] t / pavamānādibhyaḥ uttarataḥ sakṛt sakṛd avadānaṃ pātrāntare kṛtvā juvhāṃ prakṣipya / pañcāvattīnāṃ dvir dvir iti(va)d[19] eva dvir abhighāraṇam ek[20]apratyavāyaṃ svi(ṣṭa)kṛto dviś cābhighāraṇam / na kṣatābhyaṅgaḥ / anatikramaṇaṃ ca / juhotisthāne upaviśya / ājyasthālyāḥ[21] sruvāhutīr upahomaṃ juhoti / *pavamānaḥ suvarjanaḥ pavitreṇa vicarṣaṇiḥ / yaḥ potā sa punātu mā* (TBr. I.iv.8.1) *svāhā //1// idaṃ pavamānāya suvarjanāya pavitrāya vicarṣaṇe potre na mama / punantu mā.devajanāḥ punantu manavo dhiyā / punantu viśva āyavaḥ* (TBr. I.iv.8.1) *svāhā idaṃ devajana-manuviśvāyubhyo na mama //2// jātavedaḥ pavitravat pavitreṇa punāhi mā / śukreṇa deva dīdyad a* [9A] *gne kratvā kratūn ranu* (TBr. I.iv.8.1) *svāhā / idaṃ jātavedase'gnaye na mama //3// yat te pavitram arciṣy agne vitatam antarā / brahma tena punīmahe* (TBr. I.iv.8.2) *svāhā / idam agnaye na mama //4// ubhābhyāṃ deva savitaḥ pavitreṇa savena ca / idaṃ brahma punīmahe* (TBr. I.iv.8.2) *svāhā / idaṃ devāya savitre brahmaṇe na mama //5// vaiśvadevī punatī devy āgād yasyai bahvīs*[22] *tanuvo vītapṛṣṭhāḥ*[23] */ tayā madantaḥ sadhamādyeṣu vayaṃ syāma patayo rayīṇāṃ* (TBr. I.iv.8.2) *svāhā / idaṃ vaiśvadevyai punatyai na mama //6// vaiśvānaro raśmibhir mā punātu vātaḥ prāṇeneṣiro mayobhūḥ / dyāvāpṛthivī payasā payobhir ṛtāvarī yajñiye mā punītāṃ* (TBr. I.iv.8.3) *svāhā / idaṃ vaiśvānaravāteṣiradyāvāpṛthivyṛtāvarībhyo na ma* [9B] *ma //7// bṛhadbhiḥ savitas tṛbhir varṣiṣṭhair deva manmabhiḥ / agne dakṣaiḥ punāhi mā* (TBr. I.iv.8.3) *svāhā / idaṃ savitre'gnaye na mama //8// / yena devā apunata yenāpo divyaṃ kaśaḥ / tena divyena brahmaṇedaṃ brahma punīmahe* (TBr. I.iv.8.3) *svāhā / idaṃ brahmaṇe na mama //9// yaḥ pāvamānīr adhyety ṛṣibhiḥ sambhṛtaṃ*[24] *rasam / sarvaṃ sa pūtam aśnāti svaditaṃ mātariśvanā* (TBr. I.iv.8.4) */ svāhā / idaṃ pāvamānībhyo na mama //10// pāvamānīr yo adhyety ṛṣibhiḥ sambhṛtaṃ rasam / tasmai sarasvatī duhe kṣīraṃ sarpir*[25] *madhūdakaṃ* (TBr. I.iv.8.4) *svāhā / idaṃ pāvamānībhyo na mama //11// pāvamānīḥ svastyayanīḥ sudughā hi payasvatīḥ / ṛṣibhiḥ* *sambhṛto raso brāhmaṇeṣv amṛtaṃ hitaṃ* (TBr. I.iv.8.4) *svāhā / idaṃ pā* [10A] *vamānībhyo na mama //12// pāvamānīr diśantu na imaṃ lokam atho amum / kāmānt samardhayantu no devīr devaiḥ samā bhṛtāḥ* (TBr. I.iv.8.5) *svāhā / idaṃ pāvamānībhyo na mama //13// pāvamānīḥ svastyayanīḥ sudughā hi ghṛtaścutaḥ / ṛṣibhiḥ sa(m)bhṛto raso brāhmaṇeṣv amṛtaṃ hitaṃ* (TBr. I.iv.8.4) */ svāhā / idaṃ pāvamānībhyo na mama //14// yena devāḥ pavitreṇātmānaṃ punate sadā / tena sahasradhāreṇa pāvamānyaḥ punantu mā* (TBr.I.iv.8.6) *svāhā / idaṃ pāvamānībhyo na mama //15// prājāpatyaṃ p avitraṃ śatodyāmaṃ hiraṇmayam / tena brahmavido vayaṃ pūtaṃ brahma punīmahe* (TBr. I.iv.8.6) *svāhā / idaṃ brahmaṇe na mama //16// indraḥ sunītī saha mā punātu somaḥ*[26] *svastyā varuṇaḥ samīcyā / yamo rājā pramṛ* [10B] *ṇābhiḥ punātu mā jātavedā morjayantyā punātu* (TBr. I.iv.8.6) *svāhā / idam indrādibhyaḥ sunītyādibhyo na mama /* atha vā *idam indrāya sunītyā sahitāya somāya svastyā sahitāya varuṇāya samīcyā sahitāya yamāya rājñe pramṛṇābhiḥ sahitāya jātavedasa ūrjayantyā sahitāya na mama //17//* tataḥ atikramyāśrāvyāhā*gniṃ sviṣṭakṛtaṃ yaja / ye3 ya(jāma)he'gniṃ sviṣṭakṛtam ayāḍ agnir agneḥ priyā dhāmāny ayāṭ*[27] *somasya priyā dhāmāny ayāḍ agneḥ pavamānasya priyā dhāmāny ayāṭ /* upāṃ(śu) *sarasvatyāḥ priyāyāḥ* uccaiḥ *priyā dhāmāny ayāḍ agneḥ pāvakasya priyā dhāmāny ayāṭ /* upāṃ(śu) *savituḥ satyaprasavasya* uccaiḥ */ priyā dhāmāny ayā* [11A] *ḍ agneḥ śuceḥ priyā dhāmāny ayāṭ /* upāṃ(śu) *vāyor niyutvataḥ* uccaiḥ *priyā dhāmāny ayāḍ agner vratapateḥ priyā dhāmāny ayāṭ /* upāṃ(śu) *viṣṇoḥ śipiviṣṭasya* uccaiḥ */ priyā dhāmāny ayāḍ agner vaiśvānarasya priyā dhāmāny ayāṭ /* upāṃ(śu) *dadhikrāvṇaḥ /* uccaiḥ *priyā dhāmāny ayāḍ devānā(m ājyapānāṃ priyā dhāmāni yakṣad agner hotuḥ priyā dhāmāni yakṣat svaṃ mahimānam ā yajatām ejyā iṣaḥ kṛṇotu so adhvarā jātavedā) juṣatāṃ havir* (Hautrika 1.4.21) *mārjālyo mṛjyate sve damūnāḥ / kavipraśasto atithiḥ śivo naḥ / sahasraśṛṅgo vṛṣabhas tadojā viśvān agne sahasā prāsy anyān* (ṚV.v.1.8) *vauṣaṭ / idam agnaye sviṣṭakṛte na mama /* prathamapuroḍāśasyaiva prāśitrāya dānam / prasiddheḍa / anvāhāryam āsādya śatamānaṃ hiraṇyaṃ dadāti yajamānaḥ / *prajāpater bhāgo'sy ū(rjasvān payasvān prāṇāpānau me pāhi samānavyānau me pāhy udānavyānau me pāhy ūrg asy ūrjaṃ mayi dhehy akṣitir asi mā me kṣeṣṭhāmutrāmuṣmin loka i)ha ca* (KŚS. iii.4.30) / a [11B] syāḥ pavitreṣṭeḥ samṛdhyartham *ayaṃ va odanaḥ / idaṃ vaḥ śatamānaṃ hiraṇyaṃ ca brahmādibhyo ṛtvigbhyaḥ samavibhāgenāhaṃ sampradade* / bra(hmā) / ho(tā) / a(dhvaryuḥ)/ ā(gnīdhraḥ) (cf.KID. p.76) / *dyaus tvā dadātu pṛthivī tvā pratigṛhṇātu*[28] (PGS. III.15.21) / *ko'dāt kasmā (adāt kāmo'dāt kāmāyādāt / kāmo dātā kāmaḥ pratigrahītā kāmaita)t te* (VS. 7.48) / ity eva pratigṛhṇīyāt / vyūhane / *agneḥ pavamānasya sarasvatyāḥ priyāyā agneḥ*[29] *pāvakasya savituḥ satyaprasavasyāgneḥ śucer vāyor niyutvato'gner vratapater viṣṇo(ḥ) śipiviṣṭasyāgner vaiśvānarasya dadhikrāvṇa*[30] *ujji(tim anūjjayatv ayaṃ yajamāno vājasyainaṃ prasavena prohā)mi* (cf. KŚS. III.5.17-19) / *agniḥ pavamānaḥ sarasvatī priyāgniḥ pāvaka(ḥ) savitā satyaprasavo'gniḥ śucir vāyur niyutvān*[31] *agnir vratapatir viṣṇuḥ śipiviṣṭo'gnir vaiśvānaro*[32] *dadhikrāvā*[33] *tam apanudantu (yam ayaṃ yajamāno dveṣṭi yaś cainaṃ dveṣṭi vājasyainaṃ prasavenāpohā)mi* / atha sūktavāke / ā [12A] jyabhāgānte / *agniḥ pavamāna idaṃ havir ajuṣatāvīvṛdhata maho jyāyo'kṛta* (Hautrika 1.8.1) / upāṃ(śu) / *sarasvatī priyā* / uccaiḥ / *idaṃ haviḥ* / upāṃ(śu) *ajuṣatāvīvṛdhata*[34]/ uccaiḥ *maho jyāyaḥ* / upāṃ(śu) *akṛta / agniḥ pāvaka*[35] *idaṃ haviḥ* / ...... *(a)kṛta* / upāṃ(śu) *savitā satyaprasavaḥ* / uccai(r) *idaṃ (ha)vi (ḥ*..... upāṃśu *a)kṛta / agniḥ śucir i(daṃ* .... *a)kṛta* / upāṃ(śu) *vāyur*[36] *niyutvān / idaṃ (*..... upāṃśu *a)kṛta / agnir vratapatir i(daṃ* ..... *a)kṛta* / upāṃ(śu) *viṣṇuḥ śipiviṣṭaḥ / idaṃ (*... upāṃśu a)*kṛta / agnir vaiśvānara idaṃ (*..... *a)kṛta* / upāṃ(śu) *dadhikrāvā* / uccaiḥ *idaṃ (*.... upāṃśu *a)kṛta / devā ājyapā (ājyam ajuṣantāvīvṛdhanta maho jyāyo'krata / agnir hotreṇedaṃ havir ajuṣatāvīvṛdhata maho jyāyo'kṛta / asyām ṛdhed dhotrāyāṃ devaṅgamāyām āśāste'yaṃ yajamāno'sau)* ityādi samānaṃ karmāpatnīsaṃyājāt / antarddhānam apanīyānantaraṃ prā(g) gṛhapatiyāgāt[37] / [12B] sruvāhutīr upajuhoti

/ oṃ yad devā devaheḍanaṃ devāsaś cakṛmā vayam / ādityās tasmān mā muñcatartasyartena mām uta svāhā / idaṃ devebhya ādityebhyo na mama //1// devā jīvanakāmyā yad vācānṛtam ūdima / agnir mā tasmād enaso gārhapatyaḥ pra muñcatu / duritā yāni cakṛma karotu mām anenasaṃ svāhā / idam agnaye gārhapatyāya na mama //2// ṛtena dyāvāpṛthivī ṛtena tvaṃ sarasvati[38] */ ṛtān mā muñcatāṃhaso yad anyakṛtam ārima / svāhā / idaṃ dyāvāpṛthivībhyāṃ sarasvatyai na mama //3// sajātaśaṃsād uta vā jāmiśaṃsā(j)jyāyasaḥ śaṃsād uta vā kanīyasaḥ / anājñātaṃ devakṛtaṃ yad enas tasmā(t) tvam a* **[13A]** *smān jātavedo mumugdhi svāhā / idaṃ jātavedase na mama //4// yad vācā yan manasā bāhubhyām ūrubhyām aṣṭhīvadbhyāṃ*[39] *śiśnair yad anṛtaṃ cakṛmā vayam / agnir mā tasmād enaso gārhapatyaḥ pra muñcatu / duritā yāni cakṛma karotu mām anenasaṃ svāhā / idam agnaye gārhapatyāya na mama //5// yad dhastābhyāṃ cakara kilbiṣāṇy akṣāṇāṃ vagnum upa jighnamānaḥ / dūrepaśyā ca rāṣṭrabhṛc ca tāny apsarasāv anudattām ṛṇāni svāhā / idaṃ dūrepaśyārāṣṭrabhṛdbhyām apsarobhyāṃ na mama //6// adīvyann ṛṇaṃ*[40] *yad aham cakāra / yad vādāsyant saṃ jagārā janebhyaḥ / agnir mā tasmād enaso gārhapatyaḥ pra muñcatu / duritā yāni cakṛma karotu mām anenasaṃ svāhā /* **[13B]** *idam agnaye gārhapatyāya na mama //7// yan mayi mātā garbhe saty enaś cakāra yat pitā / agnir mā tasmād enaso gārhapatyaḥ pra muñcatu / duritā yāni cakṛma karotu mām anenasaṃ svāhā / idam agnaye gārhapatyāya na mama //8// yad āpipeṣa mātaraṃ pitaraṃ putraḥ pramudito dhayan / ahiṃsitau pitarau mayā tat tad agne anṛṇo bhavāmi svāhā / idam agnaye na mama //9// yad antarikṣaṃ pṛthivīm uta dyāṃ yan mātaraṃ pitaraṃ vā jihiṃsima / agnir mā tasmād enaso gārhapatyaḥ pra muñcatu / duritā yāni cakṛma karotu mām anenasaṃ svāhā / idam agnaye gārhapatyāya na mama //10// yad āśasā niśasā yat parāśasā yad enaś cakṛmā nūtanaṃ yat purāṇam /* **[14A]** *agnir mā tasmād enaso gārhapatyaḥ pra muñcatu / duritā yāni cakṛma karotu mām anenasaṃ svāhā / idam agnaye gārhapatyāya na mama //11// ati krāmāmi duritaṃ yad eno jahāmi ripraṃ parame sadhasthe / yatra*

yanti sukṛto nāpi duṣkṛtas tam ā rohāmi sukṛtāṃ nu[41] *lokaṃ svāhā / idam agnaye na mama //12// trite devā amṛjataitad enas trita etan manuṣyeṣu māmṛje / tato mā yadi kiñcid ānaśe'gnir mā tasmād enaso gārhapatyaḥ pra muñcatu duritā yāni cakṛma karotu mām anenasaṃ svāhā / idam agnaye gārhapatyāya na mama //13// divi jātā apsu jātā yā jātā oṣadhībhyaḥ / atho yā agnijā āpas tā naḥ śundhantu śundhanīḥ svāhā /* [14B] *idam adbhyaḥ śundhanībhyo na mama //14// yad āpo naktaṃ duritaṃ carāma yad vā divā nūtanaṃ yat purāṇam / hiraṇyavarṇās tata utpunīta naḥ svāhā / idam adbhyo hiraṇyavarṇābhyo na mama //15// imaṃ me varuṇa śrudhī havam adyā ca mṛḍaya*[42] */ tvām avasyur ā cake svāhā / idaṃ varuṇāya na mama //16// tat tvā*[43] *yāmi brahmaṇā vandamānas tad ā śāste yajamāno havirbhiḥ / aheḍamāno*[44] *varuṇeha bodhy uruśaṃsa mā na āyuḥ pra moṣīḥ svāhā / idaṃ varu(ṇā)ya na mama //17// tvaṃ no agne varuṇasya vidvān devasya heḍo'va yāsisīṣṭhāḥ / yajiṣṭho vahnitamaḥ*[45] *śośucāno viśvā dveṣāṃsi pra mumugdhy asmat / svāhā / idam agnīvaruṇābhyāṃ na mama //18// sa tvaṃ no* [15A] *agne 'vamo bhavotī nediṣṭho asyā uṣaso vyuṣṭau / ava yakṣva no varuṇaṃ rarāṇo vīhi mṛḍīkaṃ suhavo na edhi svāhā / idam agnīvaruṇābhyāṃ na mama //19// tvam agne ayāsy ayā san manasā hitaḥ / ayā san havyam ūhiṣe'yā no dhehi bheṣajaṃ* (TBr. III.7.12) *svāhā / idam agnaye na mama //20//* tato gṛhapatiyāgādi brāhmaṇatarpaṇāntā iṣṭiḥ śeṣaṃ paurṇamāsavat / iti pavitreṣṭiḥ samāptā[46] /

NOTES

1. parvaṇī 2. °viṃśati 3. °ntī 4. yevā° 5. °trye° 6. °ṣṭi° 7. °yakṣa° 8. priyā 9. niyutvataṃ 10. yakṣe 11. nirddeśaḥ 12. āhutetyādi 13. sevati 14. priyāḥ 15. sarasvatī 16. ddevān 17. tavasamatavīyān 18. prayātuṣṭa 19. °ritidevaḥ 20. yeka° 21. °sthālyāt 22. yasyaiva bavhīs 23. vītapṛṣṭāḥ 24. sabhṛtaṃ 25. sarpi 26. soma 27. ayāṃ 28. °gṛṇhāti 29. priyāyāgneḥ 30. °krāvṇor 31. niyutvānn 32. °nara 33. °krāvās 34. °vīvṛvṛdhata 35. pavamāna 36. vāyo 37. grahapati° 38. sarasvatī 39. aṣṭivadbhyāṃ 40. adivyaṃ nṛṇaṃ 41. sukṛtānnu 42. mṛḍayā 43. tatvā 44. aheḷamānā 45. vanhitamaḥ 46. samāptaḥ

Bibliography

I Abbreviations

BaudhŚS.	=	*Baudhāyanaśrautasūtra*
KHP	=	*Kātyāyana Hautra Pariśiṣṭa*
KID.	=	*Kātīyeṣṭidīpaka (page)*
KŚS.	=	*Kātyāyanaśrautasūtra.*
PGS.	=	*Pāraskaragṛhyasūtra*
PIP.	=	*Pavitreṣṭiprayoga (folio and line)*
ṚV.	=	*Ṛgveda*
ŚatBṛ	=	*Śatapathabrāhmaṇa*
ŚK.	=	*Śrautakośa (volume, part, page)*
TBr.	=	*Taittirīyabrāhmaṇa*
TS.	=	*Taittirīyasaṃhitā*
VS.	=	*Vājasaneyisaṃhitā*

II Texts and Translations

Baudhāyanaśrautasūtra Vol. I. W. Caland (ed.). Calcutta, 1904.

Hautrika (Kātyāyana Hautra Pariśiṣṭa). C. G. Kashikar (ed.). Tilak Maharashtra Vidyapeeth, Pune, 1984.

Kātyāyanaśrautasūtra. A. Weber (ed.). Berlin, 1854.

Pāraskaragṛhyasūtra. Gangadhar Bakre (ed.). (Reprint), Gujrati Printing Press, Bombay, 1970.

Pavitreṣṭiprayogaḥ. MS in Bhandarkar Oriental Research Institute, Pune, MS No. 422 of 1883-84.

Ṛgveda. R. Griffith (trans.). *Hymns of the Ṛgveda.* (New Revised edn.) Motilal Banarsidass, Delhi, 1973.

Śatapathabrāhmaṇa. A. Weber (ed.). (Reprint), Chowkhamba Sanskrit Series No. 96, Varanasi, 1964.

Śukla Yajurveda. R. Griffith (trans.). *The White Yajurveda*, Benaras, 1927.

Taittirīyabrāhmaṇa. A. Mahadevshastri and L. Shrinivasacharya (ed.). (Reprint), Motilal Banarsidass, Delhi, 1985.

Taittirīyasaṃhitā. E. Roe and E. B. Cowell (ed.). Bibliotheca Indica, Calcutta, 1860.

Taittirīyasaṃhitā Part I. A. B. Keith (trans). *The Veda of the Black Yajurveda*. H.O.S. Vol. 18, Massachusetts, 1914.

Vājasaneyisaṃhitā. Jagadishlal Shastri (ed.). Motilal Banarsidass, Delhi, 1971.

Vārāhaśrautasūtra. W. Caland and Raghuvira (ed.). Delhi, 1971.

III Secondary Sources

Dandekar, R.N. (ed.). *Śrautakośa* Vol. I (English Section), Part I. Vaidika Saṃśodhana Maṇḍaḷa, Pune, 1958.

Dharmadhikari, T.N. (ed.). *Yajñāyudhāni*. Vaidika Saṃśodhana Maṇḍaḷa, Pune, 1989.

Kane, P.V. *History of Dharmaśāstra* Vol. II, Part I. Bhandarkar Oriental Research Institute, Pune, 1941.

Kashikar, C.G. *et al. Śrautakośa* Vol. I (Sanskrit Section). Pune, 1958.

Nityānanda Parvatīya. *Kātīyeṣṭidīpakaḥ*. Benaras, 1924.

Tachikawa, M. *An Ancient Indian Homa Ritual* (Part I). Nagoya University, Nagoya, 1985.

Index

tracing 12, 92, 93.
Triṣṭup 172.
Trita 188.
truth 186.
Tvaṣṭṛ 19.
udakaśānti iii.
Udgātṛ 4.
ulūkhala 10, 44, 72.
upabhṛt 13, 16, 19, 42, 47, 99, 105, 122, 127, 128, 130, 131, 154, 156, 161.
upahoma 7, 17, 18, 22, 27, 141-143, 175.
upāṃśu 180, 186.
upāṃśu deities 185.
upavasatha 4, 5, 176.
upaveṣa 42, 47, 77, 78.
Ūrjayantī 178, 185.
utkara 12, 89, 90, 152.
Vādhūla Śrautasūtra ii.
Vaiśvadevī Punatī, 184.
Vaiśvānara Vāteśira 184.
Vaiśvānarī 176.
Vārāha 157.
Varuṇa 178, 185, 189.
vauṣaṭ, (also vau3ṣaṭ)16, 129, 181-183, 185.
Vāyu 74, 109.
Vāyu Niyutvat 17, 177, 180-182, 185.
veda 5, 112, 142.
vedi 11, 12, 39, 64.
vedikaraṇa 6, 10, 25, 87.
vikṛti 3, 5.
vikṛtiyāga 175.
Viṣṇu 20, 113, 172.
Viṣṇukrama 20, 28, 172.
Viṣṇu Śipiviṣṭa 17, 140, 177, 180-183.
Viśvāyu 184.
vitalization of the fire 6, 8, 24, 56-58.
vow 7, 20 26, 28, 114, 173, 177.
vratagrahaṇa 26, 114.
Vrātapatī 176
Vratavisarga 28, 173.
water 6, 8-10, 13, 14, 24, 28, 67-71, 79, 90, 94, 95, 102, 113, 114, 152, 155, 171, 178.
water-pot 166.
wife 4, 12, 13, 19, 37, 39, 72, 73, 86, 94, 96, 97, 114, 162, 163.
winnowing basket 9, 65, 66, 73, 74.
wooden scraper 92.
wooden sticks 24, 49, 50, 51, 56, 108.
wooden stirring stick 18.
wooden sword 12, 15, 87, 88, 93, 94, 114, 121, 124.
yajamāna 23, 37.
yajanīya 4.
yajñopavīta 13, 32.
yājyā 16, 181-183, 185.
yama 178, 185.
yoke-haltar 96.